CHRISTY BROWN'S WOMEN

A BIOGRAPHY DRAWING ON HIS LETTERS

INCLUDES THE FOUNDING OF CEREBRAL PALSY IRELAND
BY
ROBERT COLLIS

Anthony J. Jordan

Westport Books

Acknowledgements

I would like to thank the many people who have assisted this work. In particular I thank Katriona Maguire, the late Dr. Patricia Sheehan, the late Captain. J. Feehan, Dr. Mary O'Donnell, Peter Sheridan, Zoltan Collis for giving me access to their letters from Christy Brown. I thank Dr. Sheehan, Katriona Maguire, Ann Jones, Mona Byrne, Sean Brown, Thomas Delanty and Dr. Mary O'Donnell for giving me lengthy interviews. I thank Christopher Nolan for permission to quote his poem on Christy Brown. I thank the late Fr. Joe Dunn, Matthew Walsh,Katriona Maguire, Sean Brown, St. Michael's House, Mary Brown for photographs. I want to thank Mary Brown for permission to use the letters and other writings of her late husband and for her encouragement and assistance with this project over several years. I thank Deirdre Walsh for reading the text. Thanks are also due to Librarians, Mary Kelligher of the R.D.S., Gretta Kehoe at the Pembroke, Maire Kennedy of the Gilbert, Terry Millar of Ringsend. I thank Michelle White, Desmond Rushe, Michael O'Connor, Eamonn Mc Goldrick and David Bolger. I thank my family, Mary, Judith, Fiona (and Murphy) for putting up with this project for so long.

This book has been supported by the Central Remedial Clinic, Cerebral Palsy Ireland, Dublin Corporation and Zoe Developments.

Editor Judith Jordan.

ISBN 0 9524447 3 9

Published by Westport Books, Dublin 4.

THIS BOOK IS DEDICATED TO THE MEMORY OF THE FOLLOWING PEOPLE:

Declan Killeen, Keith Hackett, Niamh Coughlan, Donnchada Walsh, Stephen Cruise, Niall Culligan, Michael Byrne, Rebecca O'Neill, Angela Boylan, Anne Marie Kiernan, Suzanne O'Dwyer, Nicola Duff, Eva Gannon, Ann Patricia Daly, Mary Kiernan, Joan Mary Murphy, Helena Murphy, Ann Perry, Michelle Haide, Susan Shorthall, Leon Broe, Peter Howe, Stephen Conway, Thomas Byrne, Gareth O'Kelly, John Thompson, Paddy Thompson, Danny Thompson, Michael Farrell, Ken Farrell, Antonia Jordan, Keith Ryan, Derek O'Brien, Alan O'Brien, Michael Dunwoody, John O'Neill, Gary Nicholl, Mark Spandau, Robert Dempsey, Jason Scallon, David Lane, Peter Moran, Gerard Stenson, Andrew Burke, Raymond Collins, Brian Kissane, Gerard Collins, Patrick Mulvey, Rebecca Kinsella,

and

Tomas O'Cuilleanain.

CONTENTS

"A girl once told me, a very beautiful girl, that it was dangerous for people in my position to indulge in romantic fantasies...I do not see why a physical disability should preclude any romance in ones life. Life is the greatest romance of all...If I happen to be more vulnerable, more susceptible to the challenge of life and love, it is my misfortune or blessing, whichever way I meet the challenge ; either way the presence of pain will be inevitable, as a stimulant or a disaster. I will cherish my romantic fantasies, as long as I live, knowing them to be as real as anything else in life and more acceptable than the so-called realities of others. Life has made me as 'practical' as the next person, but it has never robbed me of my dreams and I am as much of an idealist now as I was in the old days, hurting just as deeply...I could no more not be romantic than I could fly to the moon ; without this romantic streak, I would be even duller and less original than I am".

Christy Brown in a letter to Katriona Maguire, March 1962.

CHAPTER ONE

POVERTY : 'A MENTAL DEFECTIVE'.

In 1932 the rebel leader, Eamon DeValera, took over the Government of the Irish Free State. Ireland had been an independent country for a mere ten years. The stench of poverty hung over Dublin. The State had been trying to find a secure footing against severe internal and external forces. The early hopes of its revolutionaries, which included Christy Brown's father, were giving way to the harsh realities of economic survival and forcing a rigid society to turn inwards. A conservative ethos permeated an almost Theocratic State. Despite the poverty, huge families were commonplace. Christy Brown's mother had 22 pregnancies and raised 13 children. A major success of the new State was the reduction in infant mortality in Dublin from 125 to 94 per thousand during the years 1923-1935.

The poor quality of housing in Dublin was notorious, with more than 65,000 people living in tenements and cottages condemned as unfit for human occupation in 1938. Dublin Corporation began to build two and four roomed houses and offered them to those families who had most children. A two roomed house cost 37% of the economic rent, while a four roomed house cost 68%. Most families were happy to escape from the clutches of rack-renting slum landlords in the city centre. The new settlements were in Crumlin, Kimmage and Drimnagh and these were without any of the essential social amenities. There were no parks, no playing fields or sports facilities, no halls, no factories. Not even schools were provided, at first. Though the new population was liberally sprinkled with people suffering from tuberculosis, there was no dispensary, no hospital, not even a district nurse was provided. The only site, suitable for a church, was made available to the diocesan authorities for a high price. The one amenity provided for the new settlers was a fine police barracks[1]. It was in this context that Christy Brown, the sixth surviving child of his parents, was born in June 1932 at Dublin's Rotunda Hospital. His mother had fallen down the stairs when six months pregnant with Christy. He was three weeks overdue when birth was induced by quinine and castor oil. He was delivered using forceps and lay unconscious for three days. Both mother and child nearly died during the ordeal. Mrs. Bridget Brown took several weeks to recover and subsequently went home alone. When she was able, she returned to reclaim her son. She was not informed that there was anything amiss with the baby. She took him home to 54 Stannaway Road, Kimmage, a four roomed house, two up and two down.

For the first few months Christy lay inert in his pram. When his mother tried to prop him up, his head fell back and his movements were uncontrolled. His muscles tended to go from looseness to extreme rigidity. His jaw would become locked as she tried to feed him. As the months passed, it was obvious to both parents that their child had something seriously wrong with him.

When he was one year old, Mrs. Brown started the process of taking him to the out-patient departments of various city hospitals. What she was told was not very reassuring. Child welfare clinics became general in Europe from about the 1920s. In Dublin there was a broad child welfare service under the Corporation, run by public health officers, but without any special paediatric training. Paediatrics had never been regarded as a major subject in Britain or in Ireland. There was no chair of paediatrics in any of the medical schools[2]. It was obvious that the baby was physically disabled in some way. But the medical men were not content with trying to diagnose his medical condition, which they were unable to do. They insisted on pronouncing that he was also a mental defective and would never amount to anything. He was a hopeless case, they assured Mrs. Brown. Though a poor working-class woman, Mrs. Brown had already reared healthy children. She was furthermore, an optimist, or rather a believer in the goodness of God. She decided to put her trust in herself, her baby and God. Her Christy was physically handicapped but she believed his mind was unblemished. She could tell by his eyes. She resolved as far as possible to treat him as she had the other children.

She succeeded in getting him toilet trained at the age of one and a half years. He also began to utter sounds. Mrs. Brown insisted his three older brothers and two sisters pay him great attention and involve him in the family activities. For the first time, at the age of two years, he lifted his head unaided. He still swallowed, however, with great difficulty. Suggestions were made to Mrs. Brown that the best thing she could do was to put Christy away, in an institution. True to her own class, she would not entertain such an idea. She was used to a hard life and she would cope with her offspring, no matter what the hardship entailed. Every spare moment she had, was spent trying to communicate with her son, trying to unlock the brain she knew was within the twisted frame. It was only while he slept, relaxed, that his contortions ceased.

54 Stannaway Road : Brown Family House

CHAPTER 2

MRS BROWN : THE LETTER 'A' : FIRST COMMUNION : THE BOWER : A BOX OF PAINTS

The Brown living-room was small, about ten foot square. It had a fire place and a round table. There was an old couch at the window, a few chairs and an armchair. There was a little kitchen, with two bedrooms upstairs. It was a tiny house but afforded a close family intimacy, in good times. The children would sit around the table doing their lessons, asking questions of their father. Christy watched everything and listened. As he got older his physical condition did not improve much. The only part of his body he was able to exert any control over, was his left foot. He became able to manipulate objects with it. He also began to use it as a weapon as the occasion arose. His sister, Mona Byrne, who was two years older, remembers that they were all " a normal family growing up. He was treated no differently. We were all treated in the same way. If we did anything wrong on Christy, the way children would fight and call names , he would defend himself. My Mother and Father would never intervene. They wouldn't punish us for doing something on him or calling him a name. But if you were out for one hour or four hours, he'd have that in his head and the minute you'd walk in the door, you'd get that left foot down on your foot so that he'd almost break it. So in that respect he was able to take care of himself".

One evening when he was about six years old, his siblings were at their homework. They were using a stick of chalk to do their sums on a slate. Christy had never seen chalk before. He got an urge to do as they were doing. He wanted to copy them. Sliding on his bottom, he approached his sister who was holding the chalk. He lifted his left foot towards her and took the stick of chalk between his toes. Everybody was surprised and waited as Christy prepared. His mother noticed what he had done and quickly taking another piece of chalk she wrote the letter 'A' on the floor. "Copy that", she said. His father had put his newspaper aside and watched. As the other children became quiet, Christy knew all eyes were on him. He tried to lower his chalk bearing foot to the floor, but failed as his foot jerked. His mother urged him to try again. After several efforts a rudimentary 'A' was visible on the floor. He had achieved his first creation. His mother knew for sure, that her faith was justified. His family realised that their brother must have some brains after all. His sister Mona explains that when the lino-pattern on the floor got worn, it turned black and was ideal for writing on.

Mrs. Brown gradually taught Christy to recognise and write all the letters of the alphabet. It was a long and laborious task, as she was a busy woman. She continued to have babies annually. Now that Christy was beginning to prove himself at home, his brothers began to take him out and include him in their games and escapades. A wooden box was fixed onto wheels and long timber handles were attached. This became Christy's mode of travel through the neighbourhood after school, as the boys went out to play, pulling or pushing their disabled brother. He became well-known and accepted in the locality, even making his own friends.

Though paediatric services were still very basic, educational services were highly developed. The Church authorities saw education as part of their mission and organised an excellent network of parish primary schools. First level education was freely available to everybody. The exception to this rule was the handicapped. Services had not developed that far yet. The authorities were concentrating scarce resources on the mass of the population. The only place Christy Brown might have got formal schooling was, if he was institutionalised, in a hospital setting. Local schools were so over-crowded that they did not take disabled pupils.

Mrs. Brown was a devout Catholic. She talked to her son about God and she taught him his prayers. Moira Lysaght, a public health nurse who visited the Brown household between 1940 and 1945 has written, in a piece about Mrs. Brown : " In time he demanded that he should make his First Holy Communion so she went to the local priest about it. He told her that it would not be possible. The boy would not understand. Seeking to lessen her misery he ended with, 'Those so afflicted are children of God'. Still the young boy insisted. So, one day the mother asked the priest himself to come in and speak to the boy himself. The priest came to the house and put the question;'Do you believe in God?' He got a quick inarticulate consent. The questioner followed up with; 'How many Gods are there?', to which the reply was 'One'. A further query; 'How many Gods are there?', to which the boy replied; 'Ah Father do you think I'm a fool ?' All these answers had of course to be interpreted by his mother, as the child's power of speech was so defective that only throaty, guttural sounds were possible. Realising that the mind was alert, the priest continued to call and give instruction until the big day arrived, when he came with the Blessed Sacrament"[1]. The question of taking Christy to Sunday Mass did not arise. But his mother did take him regularly to visit the local church of St. Agnes in Crumlin.

Christy soon began to copy whole words himself. Later he began to write words. One of the greatest thrills he got was when he produced the word 'mother' for the first time. Mrs. Brown was very happy. His grunting too became clearer and Mrs. Brown in particular was able to understand him. It was in this area that he first began to display his strong personality. When on occasion his brothers and sisters could not understand him, he would get very angry and grab a pencil to write the word. His clear message was that they were the stupid ones, for not being able to understand him. He rarely wore shoes or socks, as he found they inhibited his communication.

One of the joys of Christy's early years was the Saturday trip to the 'Bower' cinema in Camden Street. Admission was one penny or a large jamjar. Gangs of children would arrive from distant housing estates, loud, rough and bawdy. Christy would be carried in on the shoulders of one of his older brothers to join the fun.

On occasion some boy would produce a 'dirty' magazine of naked women. Christy was even more anxious than the others to see the pictures. His older brothers were then courting and Christy envied their success with the girls. He did not want to miss out on any experience.

The only black area in Christy's life and that of the rest of the family, was the regular bad behaviour of Mr. Brown. He was a moody hardworking bricklayer, who got drunk frequently and was violent at home. There were so many bodies and so little space that everyone was in danger when he got angry. As the family got older, and the children wanted to exercise their own freedom, this problem got worse. Mrs. Brown always tried to act the peacemaker, often to her own cost. During family rows Mr. Brown often recalled in anger, his belief that his wife's family felt that she had married beneath herself. He would remark, " I wasn't good enough for you ! Dorset Street wasn't good enough for the barons of Smithfield".

When Christy was about ten years old his go-cart broke down. Suddenly he was left out of all his brothers activities. He became introverted and felt for the first time, he was different from the rest of them. They were a different breed. He took to looking at himself in a small hand mirror. Soon he did not want to go out at all, not even with the older brothers. His mother was very upset with this change in him. He asked her, "Why can I not run and play like the other children ?" She replied, "Well son it's like this, when your brothers and sisters and your father and myself come to die, we will all have to go to purgatory but you will go straight to Heaven. You are putting your purgatory over here on earth". The following Christmas brought a welcome change when Christy discovered, by chance, a major interest. One of the boys had got a box of paints as a present. He was not pleased, believing that painting was for girls. Christy saw his chance and claimed the unwanted present. His mother was astounded when she saw him proceed to paint with his left foot. She got him a school exercise copy and he was able to control the brush perfectly. Painting began to liberate him from the morose state he had been in. Now he did not want to go out with his brothers, because he had something better to do.

One of Christy's First Paintings

CHAPTER 3

THE SUNDAY INDEPENDENT COMPETITION : FIRST LETTER.

Mrs. Brown was pregnant for the 22nd and last time. Before she came to full term, she collapsed at home one day. An ambulance was called and took her away. The children were very upset and the neighbours comforted and fed them. Christy wondered if he would ever see her again. The house became a sorry place without her presence. The father became even more moody and began to bring drinking companions home at night. He displayed little concern for his wife's safety, saying that there was always something wrong with her. After a few weeks the last baby was born, a boy. His mother remained in hospital, very sick. They all feared the worst.

One of the things which was most upsetting to Mrs. Brown in hospital was how the family, Christy in particular, was faring. Social workers were very few then. But the Rotunda Hospital had one. It also had some trainee social workers. As is often the case, the trainees get handed the most difficult tasks. One such person was , Katriona Delahunt, a tall elegant girl from Wicklow.

She was sent out one evening to visit the Brown household, and report back to Mrs. Brown, thus easing her worried mind. On a cold December night as Christy remembered, a knock came to their door. Mr. Brown answered. Christy feared it might be bad news. His father brought a young girl into the room and introduced her to Christy. His memory of her was that, "she was slim and tall and lovely - the most beautiful girl I had ever seen". She spoke about his mother and got him to write a note, which she would deliver at the hospital the next day.

Within a few weeks, Mrs. Brown returned home with her baby. She was still not well. The neighbours continued to help. The local curate visited, as did the nuns, who brought food. Mrs. Brown had told the whole story about Christy to Miss Delahunt. She realised from her first visit to Kimmage that Christy was someone special. She began to visit the Browns about twice a week. These visits were to turn into a lifetime habit. At that time Christy was just beginning to learn to read. Miss Delahunt brought him books and painting materials from Brown and Nolans' shop. She could not understand Christy's grunts but Mrs. Brown translated. Later as she got more used to him, the need for this lessened. She was to have an enormous influence on his early life, becoming a stabilising and civilising force. As he wrote, "apart from my mother, she was to be my greatest inspiration in the years and struggles that lay before me". Miss Delahunt was a beautiful and sensitive girl from a well off background. She brought Christy in touch for the first time with another world. She was interested in him for his own sake. She believed in him and set about providing him with the means to develop his own potential. During her visits they would spend hours together[1]. The second of Christy Brown's women had arrived. But she also became, and remained ever since, a friend to all the members of the Brown family. His sister Mona, remembers these visits because Katriona was an absolutely beautiful lady who always brought sweets or 'goodies' for all the children. "Going back to those days, 'goodies' were very precious: they were very few and hard to get".

The Sunday Independent paper, used to run colouring competitions. Miss Delahunt encouraged Christy to enter. They were for children between 12 and 18 years. He spent a long time working on his entry. Miss Delahunt later contacted the newspaper informing them that one of their entries was done by a boy using his left foot. They looked at his entry and found it hard to believe. Still, they sent a reporter and a photographer out to Kimmage to follow the story. The next Sunday, Christy had his picture in the paper as the winning entrant. The family and neighbours were very excited.

His father carried him proudly into the kitchen to receive congratulations. That afternoon Miss Delahunt arrived and kissed him on the forehead. Christy liked the taste of success. Miss Delahunt then left Dublin for one academic year to attend university in Liverpool. While there she was kept in touch with events in the Brown household, by several letters from Mr. Brown.

She recalls that he wrote a fine hand and composed a good letter, without any errors. Miss Delahunt also began to write to Christy, in between her visits. She encouraged him to reply to her. An early letter, when he was only thirteen years and she was doing her course in England, gives us a flavour of their close relationship. It shows the innocence of the teenage boy towards his beautiful mentor, as he shares the news items from home. But it also shows his shrewdness in saying things he knew she would wish to hear. It demonstrates that from quite early on the boy nurtured at least a romantic if not a physical passion for her. I give the letter exactly as it was written, except for omitting the stops which were placed as markings between each word and the use of capital letters throughout.

4·2·46 54 STANNAWAY.RD
KIMMAGE
DEAR·MISS. DELAHUNT–
JUST. A·LINE·IN ANSWER·TO
YOUR· EVER·WELCOME. LETTER
WHICH, I·RECEIVED·"O.K." I AM
GLAD YOU. ARE· ENJOYING
YOURSELF AND ·KEEPING. SO
WELL· YOU WELL·DESERVED
IT· I ·HOPE YOU'LL·GET THAT·
JOB, IN "FAIRYHILL" IT–
WOULD BE "SMASHING"
IT WAS ONLY. AFTER COMMUN-
-ION· THIS MORNING. WHEN I
BEGAN·THIS LETTER WELL
FATHER DIFFNEY·THE ·
PRIEST·WHO·GIVES·ME HOLY
COMMUNION. SAID·HE
WILL·PUT·YOUR·NAME·
DOWN·FOR·YOUR·INTEN-
-IONS·HE IS ALWAYS ASKING
FOR YOU. HE A·VERY YOUNG
GENTLEMAN. AND·HE·SAID
HE·WOULD LIKE·TO MEET· YOU
WE·TOLD·HIM. ALL ABOUT
YOU·AND·HE· SAID· THAT·GOD
WILL·BLESS·YOU·FOR·YOUR
KINDNESS TO·ME. AND SO
HE·WILL –I AM·GLAD THAT·
YOUR·SISTER·PASS HER·EXAMS
ALRIGHT·AND·THAT·YOUR·
MOTHER IS·KEEPING·WELL
HAS·MR·REDDIN·BEEN SICK?

HE·HAS·NOT·BEEN·OUT HERE
THIS LONGTIME– TONY. AND
LILY'S. HUSBAND. ARE· IN –
ENGLAND. I·AM·VERY·GLAD
THAT·YOU SAW·THE·NEW
CARDINAL·AND THAT·YOU
WERE ABLE. TO. KISS·HIS·
RING· IT·IS·A·GRAND –
BLESSING IT·IS·CARDINAL
GRIFFIN IS N'T IT? I·SUPP-
-OSE. YOU HAVE HEARED OF
THE·DEATH·OF OUR·POOR·
CARDINAL– CARDINAL –
GLEENON HE IS IN HEAVEN
NOW·I HOPE MY FATHER IS
WORKING·NOW ·AND JIM
IS WORKING·TOO·PADDY·
HAS· GOT NOTHING YET.
MY·MOTHER·GOING·ON
FINE. AND·ALL AT·HOME
BUNNY· HAS LOTS·OF–
NEW·SONGS FOR·YOU. WHE
-N –YOU COME· ALL THE
OTHERS LOVE·BEING·OUT
OF SCHOOL·I AM·LOOKING
FORWARD·TO· SEEING·YOU
SOON·MISS–DELAHUNT×
XXXXX ——— XXXXXX
X LOVE FROM ALL AT X
X HOME AND LOT·FROM·ME X
XXXX KIT·BROWN. XXXXXX
X I·AM·LOOKING FORWARD·TO·SEE-
ING YOU – LOVE

Copy of letter dated 4/2/'46.

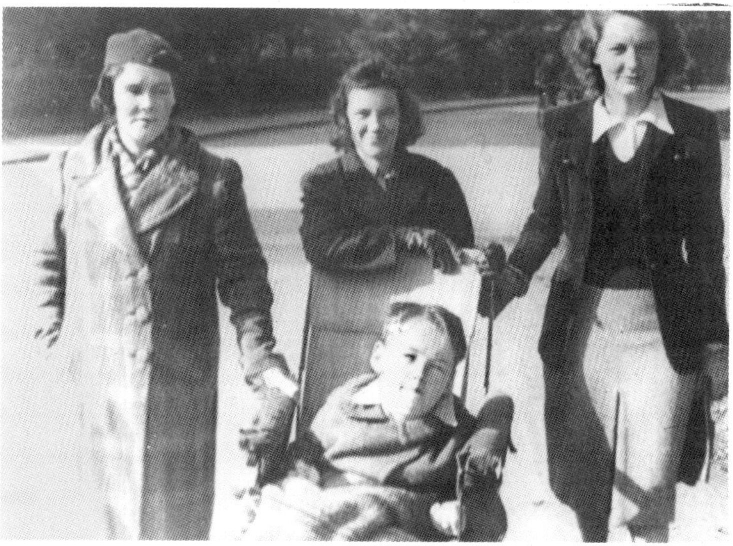

Mrs Brown, Mona Brown, Katriona Delahunt with Christy.

54 Stannaway Rd,
Kimmage,
4/2/46

Dear Miss Delahunt,

Just a line in answer to your ever welcome letter which I received 'o.k.' I'm glad you're enjoying yourself and keeping so well. You well deserved it. I hope you get that job in 'Fairyhill'. It would be'smashing'. I was only after communion this morning when I started this letter. Well Father Diffney the priest who gives me Holy Communion said he will put your name down for your intentions. He is always asking for you.

He is a very young gentleman and he would like to meet you. We told him all about you and he said that God will bless you for all your kindness to me and so He will. I am glad that your sister passed her exams alright and that your mother is keeping well.

Has Mr. Reddin been sick? He has not been out here this long time. Tony and Lily's husband are in England. I am very glad that you saw the new Cardinal and that you were able to kiss his ring. It is a grand blessing. It is Cardinal Griffin is it not?

I suppose you have heard of the death of our poor Cardinal - Cardinal Glennon. He is in Heaven now I hope. My father is working now and Jim is working too. Paddy has got nothing yet.

My mother is going on fine and all at home. Bunny has lots of new songs for you, when you come. All the others love being out of school. I am looking forward to seeing you soon Miss Delahunt XXXXX-------XXXXXXX Love - From all at home and lots from me XXXXX

Kit Brown XXXXXXXX I am looking forward to seeing you. Love

XXXXXXXXXXXXXXXXXXXXXXXXXXXXXXXXXXXXXXXXXX
XXXXXXXXXXXXXXXXXXX

Miss Delahunt got a friend of hers from the College of Art, Miss Hickey, to visit Christy to give him informal lessons. Miss Delahunt recalls his painting work: "I remember this beautiful peacock he did when he was only eleven. The control he had over his foot was amazing. He would put that book on the floor or on the kitchen table: Christy would often sit on the table inside the door: he filled in the feathers of the peacock without a single scribble, extraordinary. Later when he had his little study at the back room, that was wonderful for him because he could keep his things, his books without the others pulling at them. He could have peace and quiet. There he would sit on the bed and paint. His mother would get prepared boards in a joinery workshop for him. I remember one day he was painting the skyline of New York. He couldn't reach the skyscraper. So he just whipped it around, turned it around and painted it on the bottom. If he wanted an apple, you handed it to him on a fork. He'd take it between his toes and eat it".

CHAPTER 4

TUBERCULOSIS : THEATRICAL PERSONALITIES : VICTOR BEWLEY : MARROWBONE LANE SAMARITAN FUND : SUICIDE : A MARRIAGE .

The second world war made Ireland very isolated as it remained neutral. The war years were referred to as 'The Emergency'. In a prizegiving essay a young doctor named Robert Collis, of whom we will hear much more, wrote about the state of medicine in Ireland. He outlined the prevailing situation, particularly highlighting the rise in tuberculosis and the continuing lack of paediatric services. He urged much more centralised planning and control in medical matters. But he was not very optimistic, regarding the State as a floating log. He wrote: " Today Eire is in a very curious state. It may be likened to a log floating round and round in a back water while the torrent passes it by. On the log the ants are engaged frantically trying to maintain its equilibrium, which is being continually upset by eddies sweeping in from the roaring stream. They proclaim their right to remain clear of the general flood and manage their own affairs on their own log, unaffected by what may be happening beyond. But the noise of the crashing water has a paralysing effect. They look on, hoping vaguely for better times, but unable to act"[1].

When the State Health Authorities did decide to treat public health care as a priority measure, it ran into serious difficulties with the Catholic Church. The Church was very wary about State involvement in these matters. On one famous occasion it intervened with the government, demonstrating how carefully the civil authorities had to proceed. It wrote :

"Dear Taoiseach,

The Archbishops and Bishops of Ireland had under consideration the proposals for the Mother and Child health service and other kindred health services....In their opinion the powers taken by the State....are in direct opposition to the right of the family and of the individual and are liable to very great abuse....If adopted in law they would constitute a ready-made instrument for future totalitarian aggression.

The right to provide for the health of children belongs to parents, not to the

State. The State has the right to intervene only in a subsidary capacity, to supplement, not to supplant"[2].

There was plenty of food in Ireland during the War years, just as there had been during the Great Famine. Meat, poultry and dairy products existed in abundance. But only the well-off could afford such fare. Fruit, such as bananas and oranges were almost unknown. In the country, vegetables were grown for direct consumption. In Dublin, the poor did not realise that milk and vegetables were more nutritious for children than bread and tea.

The young doctor, Robert Collis had artistic pretensions. He spent a year at Yale, where in addition to his medical studies, he also took courses in poetry and play - writing. He used to complain bitterly to all and sundry about the poor of the city of Dublin. In his autobiography "To Be A Pilgrim", he writes that ninety thousand people lived in one-roomed tenements mostly in old battered eighteenth-century houses without proper water supply and only with communal washing arrangements. Ten thousand of them existed in basement cellar rooms, or old wine cellars. The dirt, the smell, the awful squalor that the people lived in was terrible and wrung the heart of any feeling person. Then typical of Collis, he continued, pointing the finger where he felt responsibility lay. He said that few in the upper classes knew or really cared about the poor. It seemed to be accepted that if you were born into the poor working class, your job in life was to work for almost nothing in order to support the other section of society in comfort, if not in luxury. Collis was a friend of Frank O'Connor, the writer, who was on the Board of the Abbey Theatre. O'Connor advised Collis to write a play about the Dublin slums, if he felt so strongly about them. Collis set about collecting material and planning a plot. About six months later he sat down one night and after an all night sitting, completed the bones of a play. The story concerned a girl from the west of Ireland, coming to Dublin, marrying and living in the slums. O'Connor showed it to Lennox Robinson, another well-known writer, also on the Abbey Board. They both then told Collis that his work was essentially a social tract rather than a piece of drama. Collis hoped that given O'Connor's influence, the Abbey might still be persuaded to produce his creation. But O'Connor had to resign shortly afterwards from the Abbey, when he ran off with the wife of Robert Spaight, the famous English actor. Robinson felt that Collis' play would be too controversial for the Abbey and turned it down.

Sheelagh Richards, the well-known actress and a friend of Collis', advised him to take his play to Hilton Edwards at the nearby Gate Theatre. Edwards and his partner, Micheal MacLiammoir, realised that the play had commercial possibilities, if it could be produced on stage. Together they reworked it and gave MacLiammoir and Sheelagh Richards the major parts. Collis has written that the evening before the first night, the dress rehearsal went on till 4 A.M.[3] The play called 'Marrowbone Lane' had a very successful run at the Gate. The propaganda aspect of the play moved the audience. The Irish Independent saw it as 'a blow for housing reform', while the Irish Times praised 'its intensity and truth'. The Evening Mail said Collis was 'on the side of art for truth's sake'[4]. Under intense pressure, the Housing Section of Dublin Corporation issued a statement, noting that at that very time, new blocks of flats were being built at Marrowbone Lane itself. At a meeting on public housing in the Metropolitan Hall, Councillor Milroy said that there were only 17,759 condemned houses in the city, to which Collis replied that that was an increase since 1914. Collis also told the meeting that there were only two hundred and twenty five beds for children in the city hospitals. He assured the meeting that he had not exaggerated anything in his play[5].

Out of this agitation was born a new organisation which retained the name of Collis' play, called the Marrowbone Lane Fund. Its aims were 'to feed the starving children of Dublin', through their 'Samaritan Fund', and later, to support the setting up of a National Association for Cerebral Palsy. It would be "at a meeting of the Fund held on 12 September 1949 that Dr. Collis informed the gathering that he and a Mr. Sommerville Large had formed a committee of interested people to see what could be done to help children so handicapped". The Fund voted to give an immediate grant of one hundred pounds towards the work. In November 1949 the Fund gave the large sum of five hundred and twenty five pounds, towards a premises, a part-time physiotherapist and the employment of a Dr. Warnants, as assistant to Collis.

Katriona Delahunt, who was then a qualified social worker, went to work for the Fund. They discovered that many children had contracted primary tuberculosis from their own parents who were waiting for a bed in hospital. There were no drugs to fight the disease. The treatment was lung pneumathorax and rest. Coeliac disease and rickets were common along with eye disease, caused by malnutrition. But it was clear that the main problem was that of poverty, caused by ignorance and unemployment.

The Marrowbone Lane Fund had a feeding station for children in Bewley's restaurant in Westmoreland St. Victor Bewley who was on the Fund owned the restaurant and cake shop. After these closed, the staff remained on and fed up to 80 or 90 children every night.

Miss Delahunt was involved in arranging for the children to come in, giving them bus fares. They got a balanced meal and a vitamin tablet. The Brown brothers used to come in for the dinners. Christy couldn't come in, so his dinner was sent out in a special jar which kept it hot. The Fund also gave out clothes. Miss Delahunt visited clothing factories, collecting spare materials. Quakers, at the Friends Meeting House, ran them into garments. The Fund also issued vouchers, which could be cashed at local shops. The Social Security was very low. Mr. Brown's earnings came to £4.50 weekly. Miss Delahunt visited all the families involved. She also referred any medical problems to Dr. Collis' clinic in Harcourt St. Children's Hospital, where a Dr. Epstein looked after the children once a month.

Christy had a difficult adolesence. The changes in his body frightened him at first. He had some early painful experiences with girls. These drove him back into himself. Despite the attention of his mother and Miss Delahunt he contemplated suicide and attempted it unsucessfully, cutting his wrists with glass.

With so many people living so close together, including boys and girls having to share the same bedroom, Christy was very familiar with bodies, male and female. The latter fascinated him and he lusted after them with a ferocious intensity. In 'Down All the Days', we read of many examples of how close he got to fulfilling his desires with willing females. Sex and drink were common currencies in the Brown household.

In those times people were quite formal. One always addressed one's elders and superiors in a formal manner, giving them their appropriate title. Christy had always used the name 'Miss Delahunt' when referring to the social worker. At one point he asked very seriously, if he could call her 'Katriona'. When Christy reached sixteen, his older brothers and sisters were starting to marry. Katriona had begun to give him all sorts of books to read. He devoured everything including all of Dickens. He wanted to be something in life, nothing extraordinary, just ordinary. He began to write little stories, about Cowboys and Indians he had seen in the pictures. He wrote lots of letters to Katriona. He was still feeling very isolated and becoming increasingly aware of his handicap. He desperately wanted friends but had none except Katriona. He had been passed by. Then as he has said himself, a great calamity happened. One day Katriona arrived at the house wearing an engagement ring. Mrs. Brown admired the ring and offered her congratulations. Christy was unable to do so. Katriona remembers the shock he endured that day. He was shattered, but what could she do. She assured him that her forthcoming marriage would make no difference to their relationship. She would still come and visit him. Where women were concerned, Christy was utterly vulnerable. Not for the first time nor for the last, would he be disappointed. Katriona had a large wedding at University Church on St. Stephens Green. Christy had by then acquired a wheelchair. His mother brought him to the Green to see the bride.

Katriona's husband, Conor Maguire, a legal man, spoke to Christy who was very jealous. Katriona continued to visit Christy, though the frequency of her visits did diminish. When Christy recovered from his great trauma, he again began to write regularly to Mrs. Maguire.

One such letter reads- 3/1949:

" I'm writing just a few lines in an endeavour to express my sincere thanks for the lovely file of 'readables' I received from you. There are some good detective stories among them, also some grand pictures. They shall keep me occupied for some time. I read all the weekend and I'm taking this afternoon off to write to you. The pictures are grand subjects for painting. I simply must copy as I have no other inspiration. I had a visit from Miss Hickey.

I say do you remember me telling you I write short stories in my spare time? Well I'm still at it, although I've improved since then. My latest is a Western, and my mother thinks highly of it. Read it when you come out again, won't you? I'm not bothered but I think I've come a long way from a small rather delicate boy sitting upon the kitchen table listening to the sweet voice of my teacher (that's you of course), explaining to him the alphabet.

Don't you? Although my writing hasn't improved, has it? But I know you understand it, so I don't worry. What I can't say in speech I'll say in writing, or as far as my ability permits me."

A traumatic occasion for Christy as
Conor Maguire marries Katriona Delahunty in 1948

CHAPTER 5

LOURDES : PAEDIATRICS : MEDICAL POLITICS : ROBERT COLLIS : CEREBRAL PALSY IRELAND.

Katriona regarded Christy as a very spiritual person. His early letters were full of religion. One of the longest and most beautiful she ever received from him was a ten page description of a visit to Lourdes, which she organised for him. There is a long tradition of pilgrims going to Lourdes from Ireland. In 1950 the trip cost £34. A committee organising pilgrimages put up £10 for Christy. Mrs. Brown got £5 from a relation. Mrs. Maguire organised a bridge game among her friends to make up the rest. She and her husband picked Christy and Mrs. Brown up and drove them to the airport for a 3 A.M. flight. Much to Christy's disgust, he had to endure being put on a stretcher and lifted into the plane. But he soon organised a seat for himself beside a window and was quite happy. Like many another pilgrim he started out on the pilgrimage in a sceptical frame of mind. But the place itself and the other pilgrims bore such a compelling witness, that he became enthused that he too might be cured. He prayed and prayed. He was not cured but he was reborn by the whole experience. He said of the torchlight procession, that it was the single most beautiful moment of his life. Later on of course Katriona says, he did change, writing to her at one stage saying "if I did pray, I would pray for you". He remained a sensitive spiritual man, but not with the ritual of practice.

One of the problems about places like Lourdes or Knock which raise the expectation of a cure, is the aftermath left in vulnerable people, who must return home to face the reality of their difficult lives. For Christy the experience was made all the more difficult, because for the first time he felt some invisible barrier had gone up between himself and his mother, across which she could not traverse.

About ten days after returning from France, a visitor arrived at the Browns. He told Christy that his condition was due to Cerebral Palsy - the first time the Browns had heard the term. He said that with a new treatment it could be cured, but that Christy would want to get better and be willing to work very hard. Only as the visitor was leaving, did he tell Christy who he was, "By the way my name is Dr. Collis". Mona Byrne recalls that her mother regarded this period and the visit to Lourdes as vital in Christy's life. " As my mother used to say he was never cured directly. I mean he didn't come back walking. But indirectly from the time he came back from Lourdes, you could see the change in him physically; at that stage and through a few years afterwards he started to improve; you could hold his arm and walk him, where up to that you would always have to stand behind him and walk".

Robert Collis and Christy Brown, though both Dubliners, came from completely different worlds. Yet fate would ensure that their lives would intertwine for their mutual benefit.

* * * * * *

Robert Collis was born in 1900. His birth was a difficult one and he didn't breath for some time afterwards. He was a blue baby.

He was named after Lord Roberts, a hero of the South African war. The Collis family had belonged to the landed gentry who had originally come to Ireland in Cromwellian times. By the 19th century they were writers, clerics and medical men of note.

Robert was one of twins. His mother doted on him but rejected his twin. Like his other brothers he was educated at Rugby School. He was not very gifted academically and the Headmaster there told him that he might be able to realise his ambition of becoming a doctor, 'as that did not require any great intelligence'[1]. While home on holidays in 1916, he heard of the Rising happening in the city. He cycled into Dublin daily from the family home in Killiney, wearing Red Cross armlets to witness the fighting. He saw the soldiers in the Shelbourne Hotel shooting at the rebels on Stephens Green. He helped the Red Cross bring the wounded out onto the street. At the Meath Hospital he saw Jacobs factory bombarded. He got cut off and couldn't get home. Next day his parents set off to locate him. Though the rebellion had been against 'their' army, Robert later recalled that when the leaders of the Rising were summarily executed, he suddenly realised that he was an Irishman and that he was on the side of the people of Ireland. This conversion made his father very uneasy. One of the armed rebels had been Patrick Brown, who would later become the father of Christy Brown.

As soon as Collis finished school in 1918, he joined a cadet battalion outside London to train for the Irish Guards, but the ending of the Great War put paid to that plan. In 1919 he went to Trinity College Cambridge to study medicine. From there he won a one year exchange scholarship to Yale. While at Yale, as already stated, he attended a course on English poetry and modern drama, which was to have a major effect on his future life. He returned to Cambridge to finish his pre-clinical courses before going to King's College Hospital in London for clinical teaching. There, under the influence of a famous paediatrician, Sir Frederick Still, Collis determined that he too would become a paediatrician.

Collis had endured very bad health both in Cambridge and Yale, with rheumatic fever and tuberculosis both diagnosed. But at King's College his health improved and he again began to play rugby. This led to his name coming to the notice of a famous Master of the Rotunda Maternity Hospital in Dublin named, Bethel Solomons. The latter arranged for Collis to get a trial for the Irish rugby team. He was selected to play against France in 1924. Solomons also arranged for Collis to do his practical midwifery course at the Rotunda in Dublin. Collis captained every rugby team he ever played for, except for the Ireland fifteen. He once reckoned that the bravest action he ever took, was to dive on a loose ball at the feet of the oncoming Welsh forwards. Collis, whose father had played for Ireland in 1884, received seven caps for Ireland between 1924 and 1926[2].

Dr. Alex Comfort was at the Rotunda Hospital at this time. He is quoted as saying about the Rotunda, "I remember a wonderfully Rabelaisian delivery ward where the nurse would pop her head around the curtain and tell the moaning patient to be quiet, that they were nowhere near ready yet"[3]. This was about the time Christy was born there.

Collis' spell at the Rotunda gave him his first experience of the abject poverty most Dubliners lived in. After graduating he did research at John Hopkins Hospital in Baltimore in paediatrics, after which he returned to London to Great Ormond St. Hospital. Later following his family tradition he returned to medical posts in Dublin at National Children's Hospital, the Rotunda and the Meath. He was appointed paediatrician at the Rotunda in 1932, the year of Christy Brown's birth.

Collis and his family were to be very embarrassed when he failed to pass the examination to become a member of the Irish College of Physicians. This failure neccessitated his resignation from the staff of the Meath Hospital and directed his concentration on paediatrics[4]. As he was later to direct the young Christy Brown in another matter, Collis took a correspondence course with a London college to help him resit the examination.

In the meantime Collis devoted his energies to paediatrics which were in a rudimentary state in Dublin. He became the first secretary of The Irish Paediatric Club in 1933. He developed neonatal services at the Rotunda, particularly for premature babies. This was not without its difficulty, as Collis commented that the attitude of maternity hospitals seemed illogical to the paediatrician, with every provision made for the bearing of children and little or none for their subsequent care[5]. He collaborated closely with nursing staff, in particular a Sister Moran, in the development of after-care for sick babies. He was among the first doctors to realise the vital role social workers could play in this field. To achieve his goals, he approached tasks with a completely open mind and was not hidebound by convention or practice. In 1944 he wrote " In the Rotunda we have lost the lives of 56 babies born at the hospital - through inaction. If instead of babies the deaths were those of mothers from puerperal sepsis, there would be a world-wide outcry"[6].

Collis developed a wide service in Dublin where reasonable paediatric units for the treatment of ordinary diseases of infancy and childhood were eventually supplied, but where the provision for the treatment of Cerebral Palsy (C.P.) had not yet been made. He had no special training in physical medicine and his knowledge of Cerebral Palsy was merely that of an ordinary physician, accustomed to occasional cases of 'Athetosis' which were brought into his clinic. These he referred to the physiotherapy department, without a very clear idea of what the physiotherapist should do. He could therefore issue no instructions. Collis had intended for several years to study the full facts on Cerebral Palsy, but kept putting it off. His sister-in-law, Eirene Collis, had earlier worked at the John Hopkins in Maryland with Phelps, on his new theraphy for cerebral palsy. She had then set up one of the first clinics for treating children with cerebral palsy at Queen Mary's Hospital, Carshalton, England. On a visit to Dublin, she persuaded Collis to seek to do the same in Dublin.

Collis says it was the sight of Christy Brown which finally gave him the impetus to begin his study of cerebral palsy. He said, "one day the subject was suddenly brought to his notice with tremendous force by a case which showed him the terrific drama of a human soul imprisoned within an almost functionless or at least an abnormally functioning body, yet breaking forth and apparently overcoming insurmountable difficulties. In this instance it was a boy called Christy". Collis studied the history, aetiology and treatment of cerebral palsy. One of the fundamentals of the modern approach to the treatment of cerebral palsy was that different methods had to be applied to different types of the disease. For the athetoid type, which Christy Brown had, the use of relaxation was of fundamental importance, since athetosis disappears or is greatly diminished by increasing degrees of relaxation. Following this, motion from the relaxed position is taught. Peripheral surgery had no place in this particular group.

"The earlier treatment was begun, the better was the result", Collis continued in his explanation of the treatment involved. "The scheme should be thought of as a training in movement, rather than as a series of exercises, and the emphasis had to be on the patient performing the movements himself, after an initial demonstration by passive movement. The athetoid should be allowed to work in whatever position made relaxation easier for him: this is usually the sleeping posture. Then he progresses to sitting over the edge of the treatment table and later to standing, usually with the aid of special skis and ski-poles. When he is able to stand steadily on both feet, the patient practices balancing on one leg with the other one flexed, and only then does he try to walk. Hence walking is a late accomplishment. Speech therapy, for those who need it, follows control of the respiratory movements, and of the muscles concerned in articulation, e.g., largely those used in swallowing.

School activities must also fit into the therapeutic programme so that close team work between all concerned in the reeducation of the Cerebral Palsied child is assured. The need for special schools for these children is only too obvious. Day schools have the advantage of allowing the pupils to have a normal home life".

Once more, with his early insight into the need for educational services, Collis displayed a foresight which would lead Cerebral Palsy Ireland to become the major provider of educational services to children with physical disabilities. It soon found itself being approached by the Irish National Teachers Organisation to lobby the Government on its behalf. The teachers union had realised quite early that specialised training was required for teachers to enable them to deal with children with disabilities, then beginning to come into the educational service. The union itself had put proposals to Government and felt that support from the new Association would be very useful.

Collis was then to discover that studying the problem was the easy part of his work. Like many another social pioneer, he encountered great difficulty in convincing his colleagues and the State authorities that there was a problem to be tackled. He continued, "Having acquainted myself with the above complicated picture, the next step was to apply this knowledge to local conditions and get started. I was immediately confronted with the problem which all organisers in this field encounter at the beginning: the extreme difficulty of conveying a comprehensive picture of cerebral palsy and its needs to my medical colleagues as well as to the lay authorities. The former tended either to be too busy to listen to the whole story, or were convinced that they knew about it already, and they stated that 'excellent results' were obtained in the ordinary departments of their hospitals. The established physiotherapists, on the other hand, regarded my attitude as a criticism of their competency. Charitable organisations were put off by the extreme complexity of the problem and claimed that it was clearly a matter for the government to consider".

The reply Collis got from officialdom, when he sought State intervention, was classic civil-service-speak. It also demonstrates how and why the voluntary sector in Ireland, has had to play such a vibrant role in the delivery of services to minority groups. However in Collis' usual forthright style, he does not omit to give the graphic details of the opposition he encountered in that endeavour. He reported : "The attitude of the government officials was characteristic: as a resident clinic did not exist for cerebral palsy, no such clinic could be recognised. Eventually I succeeded, after much difficulty, in persuading a charitable organisation to give me a grant with which to buy equipment and to train staff. I sent one of my assistants who specialised in a physical approach to psychological problems, and a young physiotherapist, who has a university degree as well, to Carshalton for training in the clinic there. On their return we organised an out-patient clinic in the National Children's Hospital, Dublin, to which I am attached as visiting physician. Turmoil ensued, the hospital physiotherapist complained to the Chairman of the Board that she was being unfairly treated. The matter became so unpleasant that the clinic had to be moved elsewhere. Fortunately the subject had by now received a certain amount of general support, and the Orthopaedic Hospital Board was persuaded by one of their senior surgeons to house the clinic in their gymnasium and to give it every facility. Great care was taken to avoid upsetting the established physiotherapy staff."[7]

It had been at a children's party organised by the Marrow Bone Lane Fund that Collis had first seen Christy Brown.[8] He remembered him as a small elfish figure with a strange fey face, a boy-childish Michelangelo aura of beauty. Some years later when the Cerebral Palsy Clinic was functioning, it was felt that Brown would be a suitable candidate. Collis gives a fanciful account of locating him at home after a few weeks search of Dublin. Brown recalled that meeting and describes Collis as, a well-built man with grey-green eyes, eyes that looked into him. That visit to 54 Stannaway Road Crumlin proved a momentous occasion for both men. The world of privilege had come to visit the world of poverty and consequent disadvantage. The Browns fervently believed that their son could be cured. The answer to all Mrs. Brown's prayers might be answered. Typical of Collis, he decided that the new treatment for Christy would start the very next day. That night Christy reproached himself for having doubted that the visit to Lourdes would provide a miracle.

Collis had needed to be a determined man to get the Cerebral Palsy Association functioning. Among his main backers were the parents of those children affected. They put in the laborious work of committee meetings, seeking to interest those with money to fund the new Association. In 1951 the Evening Herald reported that, "Seventy parents gathered in the St. John Ambulance Brigade premises at the back of Merrion Square, and the Parents' Association - that title is as yet unofficial - of the Irish Association of Cerebral Palsy held its inaugural and very successful meeting. All the fathers and the mothers had children who were being treated for this too often misunderstood malady, and nothing lightens a burden like being able to share it. The meeting decided to divide the city into four sections. Each sector would have a group which would meet, and each group's first duty would be to elect two members to a central committee. The Association's aims are simple. It will provide the opportunity for parents to meet and discuss their own problems, and so help each other. And ever in the minds of the Parents' Association and the parents themselves will be the need for special schools and the money to provide them for these little children".

Later that same year, the first Meeting of the Subscribers and Directors of the National Association for Cerebral Palsy (Ireland) Limited was held on the 19th of July 1951 at 26 Fitzwilliam Square, Collis' own home. Three Directors were appointed, Collis himself, Dr. William Roche and Miss Gwendoline Barrington. A short document was circulated to inform those present of how the Association had come into existence.

It read, "The treatment for Cerebral Palsy began four years ago, when the Marrowbone Samaritan Fund Committee agreed to finance a scheme which our Chairman, Dr. Collis, started at the National Children's Hospital Harcourt Street. In 1950 a committee was formed and a daily clinic was opened by the Incorporated National Orthopaedic Hospital of Ireland in their gymnasium at 22 Upper Merrion Street, and treatment was carried out there until this year, when the Hospital was offered more suitable premises at the Iveagh Centre, Bull Alley Street, and where there are upwards of eighty children receiving treatment, and their progress is amazing. That so many Dublin children are able to get this treatment is largely due to the grand band of voluntary drivers who use their own cars to bring the children to and from the clinic.......".

Christy Brown spoke of both these latter places in the last verse of his poem on Dublin, named 'City Dweller': "Yet my Liffey dreams were just as sweet as those in a Wicklow valley, and my heart was first forged in Merrion Street and blinded with love in Bull Alley"

It was while the Association was at Merrion St that its school was informally recognised by the Department of Education. It was initially called the Orthopaedic Hospital Cerebral Palsy School. The Orthopaedic Hospital Board wished to become the patron of the new school. However the person who had negotiated with the Department, Dr. Mary O'Donnell, the Medical Director of the Clinic, stated that despite the fact that the early ethos of the Association was Protestant, the majority of the children attending were Catholic and therefore the school should be under Catholic patronage. She then became the Patron on behalf of the Association. Another Catholic, Miss Josie Reid, became the school Manager. This complication with the Protestant Orthopaedic Hospital Board allowed, almost by default, the Cerebral Palsy Association to retain patronage of its school, without apparently offending the Catholic Archbishop of Dublin, John Charles McQuaid.

Board of Management, Sandymount School 1978
From left : Dr. Mary O'Donnell, Patrick Shallow, Monsignor Liam Martin P.P., Tony Jordan, Dr. Thomas Gregg.

In July 1952 "thanks to the splendid generosity of a socially-minded individual, who prefers to remain anonymous", the Association started a special residential clinic in a house in Killiney. That person was Lady Talbot de Malahide and the accommodation was in her own house. She later made it possible for the Association to purchase the Drummond School in Bray and transfer the residential clinic. That premises then became known as the Marino Talbot de Malahide Memorial Home. In the context of both these moves, Lady Talbot, as was necessary at the time, had sought and received a personal interview with Dr. McQuaid to secure his goodwill for the new operation. When the Association later decided to seek official sanction for a school at Marino under the same basis as its other school, Dr. O'Donnell was invited to attend the Archbishop's residence. There she was closely interviewed by the Archbishop's secretary Fr. Liam Martin, "in a probing and not particularly friendly manner about my views on religion and the role of the church in education", Dr. O'Donnell informed me. An agreement was reached that the new school would have Dr. O'Donnell as Patron, and have Miss Reid as Manager, to be succeeded shortly by the local Parish Priest, Monsignor Fitzpatrick.

Thanks to the initiative of a group of parents who set up and ran the Cerebral Palsy Charity Pools, the Association was soon able to purchase a large house on three acres at St. Brendan's in Sandymount. This became its main centre and headquarters. After a stay in Bull Alley Street, it was the main centre at which Christy Brown was to have experience. Only later, when the Association's School moved to Sandymount did it emerge that Archbishop McQuaid was not entirely happy with it. Officially it remained a non-denominational school and initially the parish clergy did not get involved. Some parents had to arrange for private religious instruction so that their children could receive their First Holy Communion. As happened in other situations, the Archbishop encouraged a religious order to open a unit which would deliver similar services, in an environment which would be under his control. Some children were later transferred to this unit from Sandymount. It was not until many years later in the early nineteen seventies, that the situation formally evolved to the satisfaction of the Archbishop, when his secretary, Fr. Liam Martin, was invited to sit on the Board of Management of the school. Christy Brown wrote of the school: "In the schoolroom, those who have never been able to attend normal schools with their sisters and brothers because of their 'difference', are given an ordinary primary education under a qualified National Teacher who is specially trained for such a difficult task. They are very proud of the fact that they too can go to school".

The provision of treatment for children with Cerebral Palsy soon expanded to Cork, where local pride played a major part in the rapid development of services and the subsequent foundation of the Cork Spastic Clinic. The catalyst for this rested on the person of Thomas Delanty whose two children born in 1949, had cerebral palsy. Delanty, a Corkonian, had earlier made contact with Dr. Collis and succeeded in having his children admitted to the new residential clinic at Marino in Bray. In 1954 Collis was due in Cork in connection with his medical duties. He wrote to Delanty and instructed him to organise a non-denominational civic meeting in order to start a new clinic in Cork. Collis would address the meeting and state the case. Delanty who was earlier grateful to Collis for accepting his two boys, had little option but to carry out Collis' instructions, despite the fact that he received only two days notice. Collis had insisted that the meeting should be representative of all the city's interests. Delanty immediately approached the Lord Mayor, Patrick McGrath T.D., who agreed to chair such a meeting. Delanty was then prompted to secure the good offices of the Bishop of Cork. Luckily, Dr. Lucey agreed to send a high level representative to the forthcoming meeting. Lucey had a high opinion of Collis, having served on two Government Commissions with him. This situation enabled the merchant princes of the city to throw their weight behind the effort to start a new service, with one person promising a ten thousand pounds donation. The senior medical officer of the local Health Authority, Dr. Saunders, realising that many disabled children within the city urgently required a specialised service, also gave the project his backing. The meeting took place in the Imperial Hotel on the feast day of the Immaculate Conception. A committee of twelve was elected to bring the new clinic into being. This was chaired by a prominent local politician, Gus Healy, who would later become Chairman of the National Association of Cerebral Palsy. Within a matter of weeks the clinic opened in the parochial hall of St. Peter & Paul's parish in the city centre. Within one year it moved to a building provided by the Corporation at Grattan St. When the new school at the Cork Spastic Clinic was recognised by the Department of Education, the Patron of the school was Dr. Lucey. So unlike the situation at Sandymount, control of the Cork school was given to the Catholic diocese. In later years the whole operation, moved to a modern purpose building at Lavanagh House in Ballintemple.

CHAPTER 6

THE ROOM : REDUNDANT LEFT FOOT : DR. WARNANTS LETTER TO NOEL BROWNE : TRANSCRIPTION

Christy Brown did not get access to the Clinic immediately, due to transport difficulties. Instead Dr. Collis sent Dr. Warnants to Stannaway Rd. to examine Christy and start a programme of treatment there. This presented some difficulties as space was very limited. Dr. Warnants came every Sunday. He insisted that the living room be cleared of all bodies save his patient and Mrs. Brown. Even so, that room was still too small for proper functioning. There was a garden in the back. Mrs. Brown decided that a room for Christy should be built there. Her family, apart from Christy, were not at all enthusiastic. Good reasons were put forward against the scheme. They could not afford it, they would not get approval from the Corporation. Mrs. Brown raised some money and ordered a load of blocks. She felt sure that her bricklaying husband and sons would commence work. Mr. Brown refused to have anything to do with it and ordered her to have the blocks removed from the front garden. She said she would do no such thing, and if she had to, would do the job herself. All the family laughed at this, except Christy. He longed for a room of his own. His mother set about the work herself.

When the men of the house returned the next evening from their work, they discovered that the first row of blocks had been laid. The bricklayers thought it hilarious that she had not known that a foundation was necessary first. But her initiative made them realise that the job had to be done. Little by little, as the finances allowed, the room was built. Christy was appointed foreman and indicated how the room should be laid out, to suit him best. The original purpose of the room was quickly forgotten, as Christy had it furnished to meet his living and working needs. At last he was to achieve a degree of independence.

Dr. Collis decided to send Christy to visit his sister-in-law, Dr. Eirene Collis, who specialised in Cerebral Palsy in England. He wanted her to set up a detailed rehabilitation programme for Christy. Mrs. Brown and Christy flew out early one morning to Northolt Airport. They were met by Dr. Warnants who took them to the Middlesex Hospital. There Mrs. Collis gave him a detailed examination. After this she spoke to Dr. Warnants and Mrs. Brown quietly. Then she announced to Christy that she believed he could be cured, over a period of years, if he was prepared to do a lot of work. He was thrilled to hear these same words Dr. Collis had used, back in Dublin. But Mrs. Collis was not finished. There was one other thing she had to say, which caused Christy great pain and disbelief. She told him he would have to stop using his left foot. Realising his shock, she explained that the constant use of his left foot, placed a great strain on other parts of his body, adversely affecting them. Her treatment was a total body treatment, which offered him the chance to walk, talk and use his hands. Faced with the authority and certitude of medical experts, it was no surprise, despite his own misgivings, that he assented to what was demanded. The pressure and onus to deliver was put on the patient. The Browns flew back to Dublin that same day and were met at the airport by Dr. Robert Collis. He had already got the good news, by phone from London, and was eager to commence the programme immediately.

The very next day Christy wrote to Mrs. Maguire explaining what had happened: "I am writing this letter with a mixed feeling of regret and determination: regret as this is the last letter I shall write for the next five years: determined to write the next letter with my hands. Am I mad, you wonder ? The answer is no. I flew to London with my mother yesterday (Saturday) morning with a feeling of curiosity and expectancy: last night I arrived back in Dublin with hope and determination in my heart. I shan't attempt to explain all that has happened during the past few weeks as I don't intend this to be a long letter. I will merely tell you ... I like Mrs. Collis, especially for her straightforwardness and brilliant technique. She made it very clear to me that they could do absolutely nothing for me unless I cooperate with them. In fact it is I who will play the most important part if I am to walk, talk and use my hands. They can only help me. The first task is to forget entirely that I ever used my feet. From now on I am to concentrate only on using my hands, to make them obey me. To accomplish this it is necessary for me to wear boots or shoes, not heavy, not light, just ordinary. I am also to sit in an upright position, on my er bottom, and not on my spine. In order to do this, a special chair will have to be made. I am not to slump in a chair, but always to keep my shoulders erect, not by strain or tension but by normal smooth movement. Also when I am speaking I am to keep my neck and head straight. I am also to take a deep breath when I am about to talk. To get accustomed to this I have to practise each day to take deep breaths, hold it in for a while, then let it out. Mrs. Collis explained that at first it will rush out gruff gasps. But as I progress it will come out more slowly, smoothly.

She told me - not in the medical dialect, but in simple understanding words - that part of my brain was damaged at birth, not the mental part but the part which controls the movement of my body. The brain cells of this part are damaged and although I have power to move, I cannot control my movements. In the position I use for sleeping, I must let some of the tight muscles go loose. This will mean that I get more movement I don't want. When I can do this well on my side I will go over on my back and do it there.

In a short time I will find the movement I don't want disappearing and I will be loose. I will let Mrs. Collis or Mr. Dunhoe know and one of them will see me again and give me the next steps in the treatment. Perhaps my biggest task is giving up painting. Painting is my first love and I never want to take up any other occupation. It will indeed be a big task keeping it up for five whole years...but please God the next time I pick up a brush it will be with my hand between my fingers, not between my toes. Then I'll paint your portrait. I will walk up to the door of 'Garvagh' and we will celebrate with me and my gal.

Well the time has come when I must conclude my last letter to you, or to anybody. Who knows what the dim and distant future may hold? If determination and grit has a say, it holds happiness, prosperity, independence and good-living. As far as our correspondence is concerned it is au revoir, but as to our friendship - that is endless! impregnable!".

Dr. Patricia Sheehan, who would later teach speech to Christy, felt that to ban him from using his left foot, was absolutely soul-destroying and almost sinful. She commented: "The physiotheraphy treatment in those days was based on Phelps, which Eirene Collis had brought from the States. Phelps was based on controlling large muscle groups and then getting down to finer movements. That meant you had to exercise your hips and your shoulders and then you got to your knees and your elbows and then your feet and your wrists. Christy had made his breakthrough by holding a pencil and doing things with his left foot and to be banned from doing it was absolutely soul-destroying. I know that through the years with other people. But if somebody makes their own breakthrough even though its unconventional, then to deprive them of that outlet is almost sinful, I think".[1]

The following Monday morning Christy was collected by the St. John's Ambulance Brigade and taken to Collis' Cerebral Palsy Clinic in Merrion St. Dr. Warnants met Christy and hoisted him over his shoulder into a room full of children. Christy thought there must be some mistake as he had not been told the Clinic consisted of children only. After his initial shock he recovered and gradually came to know the children as individuals. He started his treatment programme which proved much more demanding than had been his experience at home. He found it strange to see himself doing the same exercises as very young children. It dealt his ego a humbling blow.

Dr. Collis recalls Christy in the Clinic:" Christy for instance, is now our doyen, and although seventeen, is a real help to us all. He keeps a watchful and kindly eye on the activities of the younger children. His smile of approval for work well done is highly prized. This elasticity of the clinic has made it possible for us to take in some children of the educated classes. Fortunately cerebral palsy, unlike certain other crippling conditions like rickets, is not chiefly confined to the poor and the destitute who tend to be inarticulate. Hence the news that something is being done for this group of crippled children has got round, and many people have come forward with offers of help.

Public opinion seems now to be in such a favourable mood that our Committee is venturing to open a residential clinic. It appears that we have succeeded in launching in Ireland a scheme for the treatment of cerebral palsy along the most modern lines, and while accepting help from society at large and central and local government authorities, we have yet kept control of the scheme and have not allowed it to be turned into a minor department of physical medicine or a state-run institution."[2]

Through the Clinic, Christy came more and more into contact with a different class of people. They were better off and more sophisticated than he was used to. It brought him into touch with a better material life, a life he decided he wanted to have as much to do with, as possible. But it also created a dichotomy, putting up further barriers between himself and his family.

One of the factors that helped Christy survive among the children was that he discovered another 'most beautiful girl' on the staff. An intense relationship developed which Christy thoroughly enjoyed. A correspondence took place which left him the possessor of thirty-two letters of affection and wisdom from a lady named Sheila Kirwan. (He would renew acquaintance with her in Boston, during his first trip to the U.S.A. in 1960).

Christy believed that a way forward for him might be through writing. Mrs. Maguire was still his main support in this area. She realised that though he was highly intelligent there was a great need, even at this late stage, for some kind of education for him. Dr. Collis suggested that Christy do a correspondence course with a London College, but this cost money. But with Samaritan Fund money it commenced.

Christy had by then begun to get his younger brothers to transcribe his writing for him. Mrs. Maguire took his stories to several outlets. She succeeded in getting the Evening Press to publish two of them. Later she was told his stories were too sad and gloomy. Nobody was interested in them. Katriona understood the difficulty as Christy had adopted a ridiculous style, terribly pedantic and stylized. She took me through one such letter to her which illustrated this artificiality.

"I know that I have always been very imaginative and aspiring even at a time when such mundane matters were abnormally advanced especially in such a diminutive creature such as myself. I'm still ambitious; indeed that trait of nature, far from declining has increased as the charm of childish dreams has diminished by the practical outlook of manhood, if I may lay claim to such an estate. Whereas before I merely dreamed of such fantasies as they then were. I now realise the truth, that it is the most futile of all human futilities, that is to live entirely in dreams: ridiculous to spend a lifetime wistfully philosophizing about life and it's numerous peculiarities, indulging in mental generalisations about the things that go to make life. The first great thirst of mind is satisfaction. A sensitive mind will always strive to expand and enlarge the scope of activity, will always feel the want of finer cultivation and the need for liberation from the inferior mentalities that surround it. It longs with the consummate passion to answer it's right to a more dignified life, a more worthwhile destiny. It yearns for a more reasonable opportunity to ensure the full maturity of it's eventual evolution. (In interview, Katriona interposes ' a twelve year old would have been taking this dictation . How they did it , I don't know'). As you can see secretarial transition has been made. It's now Francis who is taking down my dictation. Be lenient with his writing. What is the gist of all this maze of words? It is in short that I want you to give me the names and addresses of some magazines and periodicals which might consider accepting some of my poems for publication or possibly an essay or narrative I would write if my poetical attempts should not prove up to the high standards necessary by the publishers".

As Mrs Maguire was reading this letter to me she had to laugh aloud several times. As it was being written, Christy was obviously considering what effect all this verbiage would have on Mrs Maguire, as he admonished her: " Don't dismiss this as just a frivolous caprice of the mind, because believe me, I was never of a more serious frame of mind than I am at present. If you can look up those magazines which you think might possibly give me a little encouragement and I will write to them myself setting forth to them my enquiries. Don't think that this effort if it does bear fruit will affect to the slightest degree on interference with my studies".

Katriona interposed that he never did complete his correspondence course, as the letter continued: "I have completed the four hours allocated to them. I have nearly six hours left, to kill as best I can, which I do by constantly reading and which I could devote to more lucrative pursuits. Just as an example I will send you presently a poem or essay which I will write especially so that you can judge it with critical detachment and give me your frank and advised opinion as I'm really serious about this. After all, a man cannot live with his mother forever. Neither for that matter can he subsist on the extraordinary generosity of his friends. So as soon as you can, post me any information or suggestions you may have to offer. Forgive me for the abrupt manner I have expressed myself, but by now I am sure you are thoroughly accustomed to my deplorable lack of etiquette of any kind. I have lots of things to tell you both personal and otherwise, but as I have to hurry to catch the post I will reach a rather hasty conclusion. I will write again shortly trusting to the extent that your magnanimity to greater elasticity by passing on above details if you can manage it at all.

Yours Hopefully ".

At the Clinic Christy was turning into quite a personage. He decided to write a narrative on the symptoms and idiosyncrasies of cerebral palsy entitled, 'Brief Explanation on Cerebral Palsy'. Dr Warnants thought highly of it and promised to have it published.

When Dr. Warnants decided to leave the clinic, mainly due to the lack of financial remuneration, Christy was very angry, as Warnants was the one who knew and understood him best; "Doctor Warnants and I have a friendship almost akin to brotherhood; he understands me better than my Mother now! Both speech and ideas and he knows and appreciates my various peculiarities and idiosyncrasies'. Christy wrote disparagingly of the Government's lack of financial support to Dr. Warnants, "in order to keep his splendid Clinic for the rehabilitation of cerebral palsied children open. He has been left to carry on this battle against the disease alone; one man against the gross ignorance of a clique of nit-wits who have the audacity to claim they have sufficient ability to govern a country. I think most of them would be better suited behind a plough in the wilds of Connemara". Christy decided to write a letter to the Minister for Health, Dr. Noel Browne, emphasising how important it was for him to be generous in grant aiding the new organisation for cerebral palsy.

Around that time too, he began a novel called - Yearnings of the Heart - about which he wrote to Mrs Maguire :

“I have endeavoured to infuse into it the ingredients that to my mind go to make a successful book, pathos, humour. I shall try to refrain from putting slobbery sentimentalism into it. It is mainly based around a controversy of contrasting beliefs and views permeating it”, adding “I will be very pleased if you will look it over, the next time you come out ”.

Christy at Bull Alley Street.

CHAPTER SEVEN

AUTOBIOGRAPHY : REWRITING : 'THE GUIDING LIGHT' : PATRICIA SHEEHAN : DAVID FARRER : FATHER DIES : ABANDONS CLINIC .

When Christy was eighteen he decided the time had come for him to write his autobiography. His younger brother Eamonn, who was his scribe, was surprised at this endeavour. But he began the regular sessions in Christy's study. Christy often had to spell out words for Eamonn, for he never used simple terms when more abstruse ones were available. Shortly after starting the new book, he felt it necessary to write a dramatic letter to Mrs Maguire, with a special request. In this letter he sings the praises of another woman, Sheila Kirwan, "one of my very best friends".

" My Study

Dear Mrs Maguire,

This is not, strictly speaking a letter. You see I have reached the stage in my book where a vital decision will have to be faced and a very important question to be asked; I hesitate somewhat to ask you this, but knowing that I must necessarily approach you on this matter, I might as well get it over with. This is it in a nutshell. Have I your consent to mention you in my book ? I can of course disguise your identity under a non-de-plume, if you wish. But please don't deny me your permission to write about the tremendous influence your friendship has wrought upon my life. It was upon the basis of our friendship that I first founded my determination to resist defeatism and capitulation to fate. I derived my inspiration from you to re-mould my life, to make a more worth-while shape. So please, if it at all agreeable to you, don't let me down at this, at this vital stage. Give me your answer as soon as you possibly can, as I don't want to waste any time proceeding with the book.

You didn't know I wrote poetry, did you? These are some that I composed two months ago. A friend typed them out for me. I have some more at home which I will show you when you visit me again soon.

What do you think of my poetical potentialities or do you consider I should adhere solely to writing silly old books? Doubtless you are wondering who the person is I loaned the painting to? I don't think you have met Sheila Kirwan, have you? She is one of the most efficient helpers in the clinic and is one of my very best friends. She is a first cousin to Cecil Ffrench-Salkeld to whom she has shown some of my paintings and poems and intends showing him your paintings. Incidentally she asked me to enquire if you were acquainted with Mr. Ffrench- Salkeld, as she has a notion you are. Come over to the clinic the first opportunity you can get and I'll introduce you to her. I do so want you to meet her. She is the most wonderful girl, with the most marvellous personality. She and I write innumerable letters to each other on various subjects, ranging from the many branches of philosophy and literature to music and art, all of which helps me tremendously in the intellectual sphere. Recently we had a discussion on the music of Chopin, who is her favourite composer. We compared him with Mozart, who is my idol of the piano. My favourite orchestral composers being Schubert and Handel. Yes, I am surely blessed in having such wonderful friends as you and Sheila. I want you very much to meet her one day. By the way, she is a graduate of University College Galway. Her home is in Oughterard.

Recently, Mr. Gallagher brought me out to visit "Marino", the new clinic in Killiney. There are about fifteen children receiving treatment, mostly babies. Its a very beautiful place, with a healthy environment. Sheila is a resident helper out there. She is a most energetic girl, working in the two clinics!

As I said, this is not a letter, as I wrote to ask you for your permission about the matter I mentioned. So adieu for now.

Christy".

The title of the work-in-progress was "The Reminiscences of a Mental Defective" and it eventually ran to many thousands of words. The exercise made Christy very irritable because the longer it went on, the more he realised how awful it was. The programme became a nightmare, but he refused to desist. He believed he had something to say, if only he knew how to put it. He knew he needed help badly, but where was he to get it. Then one day in a fit of temper, a name came to him, an obvious name, Dr. Robert Collis. Christy couldn't understand how he had not thought of him before. Though Collis had initiated his treatment at the Clinic, Christy had not seen him for over a year. Collis had handed over the work there, to others and was pursuing other medical interests.

Collis recalls that he got a telegram from Christy reading, "I'm trying to write a book. If you don't mind, please come and help me"[1]. Christy himself said that he wrote a postcard to Collis and subsequently felt embarrassed as he realised he did not really know Dr. Collis at all very well. Collis answered the S.O.S. and visited Browns. There he was shown a pile of school copy books, all hand written but legible. He knew that a great effort was being undertaken and that he had to be careful about what he said.

According to Christy, Collis read them immediately and passed judgement[2]. However in his own autobiography " To Be A Pilgrim ", Collis says he took all the copies with him and later perused them in private[3]. They were terrible, cliche ridden, old world language, full of Dickensian expressions. But as Collis read the description of the occasion when Christy first succeeded in writing the letter 'A' in front of his admiring family, he knew there was some hope. He decided to encourage Christy.

Collis returned to the Browns and true to form, gave Christy a long lecture about writing. He hoped it would do good, realising that his listener was in no position to argue back. He gave him a collection of modern authors to read. Finally, pointing to the bundle of copies, he told Christy that he would have to start his story all over again, but that it would be worth it. Christy agreed. Collis shook his hand firmly and was gone. Collis was a very formidable man who expected to get his own way in most matters. He had no small talk and got to the point at issue immediately. He was a man of action, a hard man, even a harsh one. He was an achiever. He liked to start projects and get his minions to follow them through. He respected those who tried and succeeded. He and Christy Brown had a lot in common.

The rewrite started, this time with a different brother, Francis, as scribe. It was laborious but the copies soon began to pile up again. One night Collis arrived unexpectedly for a consultation. Christy was very nervous as he waited for the verdict. Collis pronounced it better than the first effort, but still not good enough. He said it too, had to be abandoned and a fresh start made. He advised that it was still cliche ridden and too much off the point.

Collis then contacted Mrs Maguire about getting someone who would teach Christy. There were so many areas he was completely ignorant of, that had to be filled, if he was ever to be a successful writer. Mrs Maguire approached the local Parish Priest, Canon Hickey. He persuaded a local teacher, Mr. Guthrie, to give Christy private tuition one night a week. Mr. Guthrie became so fascinated with his pupil that he was soon visiting Browns several nights weekly. The subjects they covered also expanded from the original English and Mathematics to a wide curriculum which included Latin and Classical music.

The Marrowbone Lane Fund provided the textbooks. This arrangement lasted for one year until Mr. Guthrie died suddenly, of a cerebral haemorrhage.

A third attempt on his autobiography was begun again with the assistance of his siblings. Ann Jones recalls this exercise: "When we would come in from school we used to have to take dictation from him, which we hated, but we had to do it; it was part of our duty when we were growing up; one day a week; I used have to do it two days; the boys used to do it the rest of the week. I was only ten and eleven at the time. We used to have to go out there for an hour or two hours every evening. He wasn't allowed to use his foot. They thought it would interfere with the treatment he was having at the clinic. From that age I can recall taking the dictation"[4]. When I asked Ann whether they were conscious that their brother was a bit of a genius, she replied: "Oh yes, for instance, Christy would come out with such big words that you wouldn't be able to spell them. He'd get you to spell them once, and the next day I went out and was taking more dictation from him and that word came up, you'd get a kick under the table. So you knew you had to remember the word, so with the result I think I was quite good at spelling. I could spell practically anything. We used to give him a slagging over it, brain-box and what have you. He still didn't appear any different to us. It was that he was quite intelligent and then we realised he was a genius as we got older. But when we were younger we paid no heed to it"[5].

As the latest effort progressed Christy wrote to Katriona Maguire outlining his work and study schedule. Despite his grim determination to succeed and his belief that a formal education was not a prerequisite for success as a writer, he nevertheless asked her to pray for his cause. Should a transmigration of souls ever occur, he hopes for either the soul of Thomas Carlyle or John Ruskin.

" Dear Mrs Maguire,

At last I have set myself the pleasurable task of writing to you. I suppose by now you have realised what an ill-mannered, lackadaisical parasite I am. And I have no excuse to offer for my unpunctuality, except that of over-work. As a point of interest you may like to know how I spent my holidays. Here is the programme; from ten in the morning until about noon, I am relentlessly pursuing my mental education. The object being at present philosophy, mostly in the introductory stage. Then from two until about six o'clock I am working away at my book---by means of dictation of course, which makes it more difficult and tedious, both for myself and my brother, especially for the latter who has to bear the brunt of my many temperamental explosions. Not wishing to make him a virtual slave to my pen I let him go and enjoy his few remaining pleasure hours while I again take up the task of educating myself, usually until eleven in the night, and sometimes I am in the study until after mid-night. So you can see I don't get much sun! beside I much prefer the moon. On a moon-lit night I experience a deep inner tranquillity, a strange celestial detachment from the rest of humanity, almost as if I were alone on the earth and had all eternity to explore the whole revolving universe. A strange feeling, you say, but then such sensations only occur to strange people. Persons with a vivid imagination, and mine has always been acutely hyper-sensitive, but forgive me. Here have I been vainly chattering away about myself and my fantastic notions without saying how deeply grateful I am to you for your extremely prompt response to my sudden, haphazard request for a philosophical book. Need I inform you that I find the story of mankind not only interesting but also of immense help to me in my historical studies. It was indeed the gesture of a true friend, and one of many which you have made during the past years. But to me the most obvious portrayal of your friendship was shown comparatively recently. Remember the occasion on which mother took ill ? At that time I sent you a rather hysterical message notifying you of her illness and asking you to come out and see her. To any other person that message would have appeared as the work of a hypochondriac, but not you. You saw that it was a genuine appeal and came out immediately to comfort and assure me. I suppose you may have observed by now my obvious reticence to enter into any lengthy conversation with anyone, sometimes not even with the family. My main verbal output being short monosyllables, such as 'yes' or 'no'. But even if I did not express my gratitude in words, I felt it all the more, and beside I am convinced that it would be practically impossible to convey my immense thanks to you for that most kindly act in mere human words. I shall never forget that gesture. It is ineradicable, safely locked away in the secret storehouse of my mind, along with countless others. Your numerous kindness to me are indeed past forgetting. No, I am afraid I shall never be the friend to you as you have been to me. That would be an impossibility for many reasons. But the long , broad vista of the future is spread out and who can tell what an adventurer like me will discover? It may be heartening success or dismal failure. But I am determined to find out which it will be.

The book is progressing along the appropriate lines and is steadily increasing in volume. I have already completed four chapters and intend beginning the fifth immediately. I do not often ask the boon of prayers but please do offer one now and again for the success of this book. I am putting heart and soul into it. I intend writing twelve chapters, which will take about two years to complete.

Certainly it is strenuous work, but I revel in it, and my reward will be its success.

If it is a success then I definitely intend taking up a literary career. I think my theme will be essays. A subject that I am not particularly deplorable at. Of course my lack of proper education will be a disadvantage but I do not consider it insurmountable. Certainly I shall not be baulked by it. One does not have to be an Oxford 'don' to write a book. Further I am of the opinion that one does not have to necessarily possess a college education in order to gain a niche in the literary world. Still, I often wonder if I shall ever see my book in print. I showed Mr. Gallagher the first volume and he later assured me that I would have no difficulty in getting it published. Though he said 'I was inclined to be slightly pedantic'. Such is the eagerness of an awakened mind. Well, I won't bore you with my self-centredness any longer, except to say that Mother is quite well and wholly recovered. In fact she has had no pain this three weeks and indeed she even goes so far as to hope that the ulcer is dissolved and has recently been x-rayed to prove or contradict her belief. We are still awaiting the result with bated breath. I am no diagnostician but in my view her illness is a psychological one. Her nervous system has been shattered by tremendous domestic strain.

I do hope that you and the family are in the pink and enjoying the holidays. They are such a break from the monotonous routine of everyday existence, but personally I loathe them. Incidentially, what do you think about the theory of the transmigration of souls? It would be great if I had the soul of Carlyle or Ruskin. What a hope that is!

Christy

The latest effort had begun, amid fear that it might be fruitless. But Collis had to be reckoned with and Christy was very apprehensive of being branded a failure from that quarter. The older he got, the more he realised that writing was his only means of escaping from a life of total dependence. Very early on in the third draft, Christy made a momentous decision. One evening he sacked his scribe Francis, ordering him out of his study. He then tore off the shoe and sock from his left foot. He grabbed a pencil, put it between his first and second toes, and began to write. Suddenly he was happy and fulfilled again, feeling that he was back in control of his creation. It could not but be successful. He regained a sense of freedom.

Christy began to diversify and started to write plays. His second effort, dated

September 1952, was called, "The Guiding Light", a play in five acts. The dedication is not completed, though I suspect it was to Dr. Mary O'Donnell, then Medical Director of the clinic. It reads

" For ___________ . It is doubtful that this, the second attempt at drama that I have presumed to make within so short a period should enhance my meagre literary prospects. Indeed I might possibly be censured for choosing so strong a theme notwithstanding my inexperience in the domain of drama. My presumption however in desecrating the noble temple of Drama is surely eclipsed by my impertinence in dedicating so poor a work to your honour. But nonetheless I do so with the utmost confidence in your gentle compassion from one who is privileged to remain your servant"[6].

In the 'Preface' Christy writes "In the following play I hope to present as clearly as my powers will enable me, my own purely personal conception on the strength of human affection in its highest and noblest, but sorely misunderstood form, that is, love.

The love that exists and acts as a powerful force of sympathy and attraction between two people...The eventual conquest of human love over all the crushing ultimatums and terrifying force of fate...". He ends the preface "We shall see if I possess sufficient ability by which to vindicate and render justice to the subject that I have chosen to work upon, so that its nature and my purpose in conducting an exposition of it, may be fully understood and appreciated".

It was at Bull Alley Street that Christy first met another woman, who would play a major and distinctive part in his life. The young voluntary worker, Dr. Patricia Sheehan, taught 'speech'. She had earlier sought work from the Dublin Health Authority but was informed that the Corporation did not employ married women. Dr. Brid Lyons Thornton directed her to the "new spastic clinic that had just opened in Bull Alley Street". Christy became very interested in this subject and in the teacher, believing that speech held the key for true interpersonal communication. He wrote, "I would rather have an hour's fierce argument with a pal or a few moments of soft chatter with a girl, than write the greatest book on earth". Dr. Sheehan found that he had severe dysarthria, speaking as if he had a large sweet in his mouth, with poor breathing and contortions of his jaw. She quickly got used to his speech and thought his personality magnetic. "He had a keen wit and observed you closely, to see if you were understanding him. If you didn't, you were an idiot", she told me.

A memoir Dr. Sheehan wrote of this time reads: "I first met Christy Brown on 8 October 1952 at the National Association for Cerebral Palsy clinic in Bull

Alley St. The premises, donated by the Guinness Iveagh Trust was used as a clinic in the mornings and in the afternoons as a play centre for underprivileged children of the area. It was known locally as 'the Ould Beano'. Christy was twenty years old and I was twenty four. I was newly married and had come to the clinic to teach 'speech', as a voluntary worker. Christy was delighted to meet me.

Speech was the one thing in the world he most wanted to improve and he was highly motivated. He had severe dysarthria and talked as if he had a hot potato in his mouth, his jaw jerked to one side (and sometimes even dislocated itself); his breathing was very poorly coordinated. He sat on his hands to keep them quiet and he could hold a pencil between the toes of his left foot...Soon I could understand his speech and he had such a quick wit and sense of humour and magnetic personality, that within a few minutes of conversation with him, one completely forgot that he had a physical handicap, because one became so completely engrossed in communicating with him. His eyes flashed around, he was a very keen observer. If you didn't get the meaning of what he was trying to say, he heaved a sigh of relief when you did".

Dr. Patricia Sheehan.

In March 1953 the Clinic made its final move, to its own premises on Sandymount Avenue, near the Royal Dublin Society grounds in Ballsbridge. There, they had a large house and extensive grounds with gardens and an orchard. It had been owned by the Martin family. There, they were able to offer a more diverse and individual service, particularly in speech therapy. That year too saw a major development when the Department of Education formally recognised their existing school at Sandymount, St. Brendan's. This took a major financial burden off the voluntary body as it received the normal grants towards the expenses of running and maintaining the school. It also meant that the teachers were then paid directly by the Department of Education.

Christy wrote every afternoon after arriving home from Sandymount. His attempt at autobiography was by then drawing praise from Collis, who arranged that the first chapter got a public reading at a fund-raising concert. Burl Ives had come to Dublin and performed at the Gresham Hotel. All the Browns attended with Mr. Brown buying a new suit for the occasion. Collis himself did the reading, which was well received. Afterwards Collis presented Mrs. Brown with a bouquet of flowers on-stage, to the delight of the audience. Christy was thrilled to see the most important of 'his women' so publicly acclaimed. He hoped that his day of fame would soon arrive.

Eventually the manuscript was almost finished. Collis undertook to examine it for typing errors, as this would have been extremely difficult for Christy to accomplish. Collis also arranged for the London publishers, Secker & Warburg, to agree to publish it. They provided an editor named, David Farrer, to prepare it for publication. Collis threw a party to celebrate the event at his house in Fitzwillam Square. Dr. Sheehan remembers the 'Brown family choir' singing in harmony. Christy, who was euphoric over the pending event, himself organised a pre-publication party for his friends. He wrote to Mrs Maguire on 12 October 1954 : "I am delighted to know that you can manage to come to my little 'coming-into print' party next Tuesday. You, not I, will be the guest of honour. I will expect you here around five or so and we'll all go by car to Maura Laverty's house in Leinster Road, before travelling on to the Gate to see her play 'Tolka Row', which I believe is quite a classic of Dublin life, in the lower stratum. By the way, what do you drink beside tea?

The book is almost finished. I'm slowing down the pace on it, as we still haven't heard from the American publisher yet regarding the impression my first ten chapters had on them. I'm just dying to see the whole thing in print. In the meantime, I'm writing tons of poetry every time I get a chance. I've improved enormously.

Later this year I'm going to see about having a book of poems published. I think that would be the ideal time to do it, a few months after my book comes out, as a sort of sequence. Then of course there are many plays to be written. This year I also hope to write a play with Dr. Collis and get it produced somewhere. We should work well together, since we understand each other so well. I regard Dr. Collis as my Socrates - my life will be a dedication to the love I bear him.

Incidentally, I'd like you to visit me at the Clinic some day you have time. I'd like to introduce you to Dr. Sheehan, our speech therapist, who is teaching me to talk instead of grunting. She's really brilliant. Have no apprehensions - the lady's married!".

The original house at St. Brendan's

The publication of 'My Left Foot' was Christy's big breakthrough. All the family went out to the airport one Sunday morning to see him, his mother and brother Tony, off to London for the publication. Mrs Maguire was also there. In London there was a huge party to celebrate the launch of the book in the Irish Club in Eaton Square. It was attended by many notables as well as many Browns. Dr. Collis recalled the affair reaching its 'Celtic peak', late in the evening, with two inebriated waiters encouraging all to have another 'sup of the craythure', while representatives of the publishers, who were paying for everything, calling loudly to 'shut the bar'. He recalled Mrs Brown sitting on the knee of a distinguished Anglo-Irishman, but could not be sure if it was Cecil Day Lewis or Lord Longford. Collis finally got the last guest, one of Christy's brothers, off to bed by pretending he was a dog and taking him upstairs on an imaginary lead, barking![7]

The book achieved great success and he was paid well. It turned him into a minor celebrity. Collis sold the American rights of the book through his own New York literary agent. It was translated into several languages making Christy an inspirational figure for many disabled people. Those at the Clinic in Sandymount were thrilled that one of their own had become famous.

On the home front as the cash flow increased dramatically, the staple drink of Guinness now had brandy as a rival. Tony took Christy to various functions where he began to meet people he had only heard of previously, such as Brendan Behan. They travelled everywhere by taxi. Mrs Brown began to worry and sometimes wished that the money was not so plentiful. But while it lasted they spent it, enjoying life, not thinking too much about the future.

The following year 1955, at Easter time, Mr. Brown collapsed at home one night when Mrs Brown was out and the children were in bed. Coming home late, Mrs Brown heard a low whimpering sound of someone in pain behind the closed scullery door. Mr. Brown had fallen and hit his head off the enamel bathtub. He was barely conscious as his wife comforted him in her shock. Mr. Brown was removed to hospital, where Christy saw him in pyjamas for the first time ever. After a brief hospitalisation, during which Christy was shocked to see how his father's eyes "were glazed, dulled, denuded of any light, the mouth crooked and slack and dribbling", he died. In the mortuary Mr. Brown was laid out in a brown death shroud. His face looked smaller than in life, shrunken, shrivelled, though his eyebrows still reared like cliffs. As Christy gazed at the corpse he almost expected his father's eyes to open and stare up at him with all their old fire and venom. He could imagine how his father might roar at him as to what the hell did he think, he was looking at. But Christy realised that this was a dead body which would soon be rotten. He and his brothers replaced the hood of the habit over their father's face and went outside.

The Brown household was turned upside down and washed and polished and dusted with its best materials brought out for the occasion of receiving those calling to offer condolences. Food and drink, especially that of an alcoholic nature was in constant supply. Six of the family, travelled in the first carriage to follow the hearse on the way to the cemetery. Christy saw the tears shine behind his mother's veil as she sat between two of her daughters. As a veteran of the 1916 Rising, Mr. Brown's coffin was draped in the National flag. Christy walked to the grave between two brothers who supported him by the elbows, his jerking stride attracting the attention of mourners. He was determined to complete the walk to the grave and threatened one brother, who suggested lifting him along. People passed by on their way from other new graves and Christy thought they looked disapprovingly at him. He growled at them and felt the better for it, for he was not a beast under leash. As the first volley of shots rang out over the grave, Christy felt the sweat trickle down his forehead, though the weather was wet and cold. He looked at the firing party of old veterans of the War of Independence, as they knelt unsteadily on one knee and then stood erect with their rifles on their stooping shoulders. A trumpeter sounded the Last Post and the flag was removed from the coffin. As the priest finished the prayers, the gravediggers immediately began shovelling clay onto the box below, which entombed his father. His mother began to cry.

Christy was then twenty three years old. Though he disliked his father on many occasions, particularly when he was drunk and violent to the family, he never hated him. He remembered him later as a very hard man to live with. He could be brutal on occasion, but it was born out of a sense of frustration. He was angry because of the position he was in. He was a very inarticulate man[8]. Drink was an outlet for him, as were sex and violence. He treated Christy more or less like the rest of the family. He was a proud man who wouldn't ask any man for anything, not even the price of a pint. Robert Collis described Christy's father, "His father had been kind and helpful to him though he was a strange mixture of passionate violence and imagination. He had impregnated his wife twenty two times. He was often drunk. But he had a queer sensitivity and was a great worker in the building trade"[9].

At first Christy couldn't believe that his father was dead. Later he actually missed him and cried at the sense of loss, because his father could be very generous at times. Though Mrs Brown had a rough time from her husband, she too loved him deeply. Christy remembered one rare occasion when he saw his father touch her hair, almost timidly. It made him so happy and remained for him a symbol of how a loving relationship should be. Though as we shall see, he later wrote in vivid detail of the brutality of the same man to his wife and children.

Mona Byrne recalls how devoted her father was to his wife and to Christy. "My father was the type of man who said 'just leave me in the background. You do that Mrs'. He always called my mother 'Mrs'. 'I'm not able to talk to these people Mrs'. My father was a maintenance bricklayer in the Corporation stationed down on Sundrive Road. He used to go to work in the morning and he used never take his break on the job. He would make his way back up Sundrive Road around half past nine or ten. He would get Christy up out of bed and take him to the toilet and dress him and shave him if necessary. My mother always cleaned his teeth and fed him. That's why some of that film was really..".

That same year of 1955 saw Dr. Eirene Collis reassess Christy at the Sandymount Clinic. She found that his general condition had improved. But she found his speech too forced and recommended a cessation of speech therapy for several weeks. He was to continue to do relaxation exercises but movements of his hands were to be the primary concern. She said he should continue to attend the Clinic.

But Christy had other ideas. He felt that his time was becoming more valuable. There were so many projects he had in mind that he felt he could not afford the time it took, to attend regularly at Sandymount. He had achieved unaided walking, though he tended to fall backwards. He took the courageous and unheard-of step, of discharging himself from the Clinic in 1956. He explained his thinking in a long letter to his speech mentor and close friend, Dr. Sheehan: "Now comes the difficult part of this letter. My exit from the clinical scene and all that. It's not exactly easy to discuss it without being misunderstood, and least of all with one of the Staff - capital letter for that! But since I look upon you as my friend as well as my former instructress - oh Christopher! - the task is made a little easier. To put the whole thing in a nutshell - cliche! - I was convinced that to remain on at the Clinic would be a selfish and unnecessary waste of both my own and the Staff's time and energy. And my reasons for thinking thus? I simply felt I had reached my pinnacle of progress and could advance no further. Or perhaps I should say - intrepidly - that the Clinic had reached its peak of assistance and could benefit me no further. As far as physiotheraphy goes I firmly believe that is perfectly true and undeniable. No; it wasn't just a matter of time - it was a matter of purpose. The C.P. treatment at the Clinic, and all over Ireland, had a certain standard, a certain demarcation line of progress beyond which it was as yet unable to go, not because of technical incompetence, but because the entire system of treatment here was still in the initial stages. I definitely believe I had reached that standard; what I had been taught before had brought me up to it.

But my physical needs were now greater and more complicated, and a high degree of specialisation was required to meet them. I daresay that sounds horribly conceited, but I am speaking in the broadest and most practical sense and I feel sure you grasp my meaning. I think I can say I made good use of the treatment which I had received before, and it enabled me to attain a hitherto unknown amount of personal independence. But my treatment reached a point where it was all like a circus roundabout, going about and about and yet always at the same place at any given time. It was like a repeating decimal. I understand a certain amount of repetition is essential, but after six years of going through exactly the same movements and doing exactly the same things, the necessity to implant the movements on the patient's memory, to me, is a little over-stressed. These six years of treatment had moulded me into shape, so to speak, for further and more intricate treatment, but nothing happened; things just went on repeating themselves ad infinitum, like the movements of history.

A mere matter of impatience, you say? Yes, after six years I admit I became rather impatient. My only regret in leaving the Clinic is that my work with you had also to cease, for in that sphere there was unbounded scope for improvement. I still carry on valiantly athome, and the little progress I have achieved and maintained in this crude way is an indication of what I would be now if I had your help and guidance still".

This letter will strike a chord with many people who have been under treatment for long periods, particularly those in institutions. We can only admire the writer's fortitude in coming to the decisions he did, and enforcing them. The reaction from those in charge of his treatment is not documented but they were not amused, as later events will show. This is also the first of many examples to come, where Christy decided that it was in his own best interest to move on and abandon people or places that had outlived their useful purpose for him.

Christy walking in 1954.

Christy also told Dr. Sheehan that he had just finished his first narrative poem, done in blank verse. He thought that apart from whatever poetic merits or demerits it may possess, it marked out a very considerable step in his poetic development. The theme of the poem, he wrote , was subjective and through it, he had come to a deeper knowledge and assessment of himself and his own intimate problems. The technical framework of the poem was a glorification of prose in poetic form. His choice of metre, or lack of it, might prove shocking to the intellectual elite, but he really did not give a damn. The final version, which was the fifth, was much shorter than the original ones and could not be further reduced, without robbing the poem of much of its meaning and expression. He wanted it to be recorded and asked Dr. Sheehan to consider doing it. He offered to send it to her, adding that "you see I have my own little means of transport now, a neat Ford Prefect, small but comfortable. Quite a new model too. Oh I say, aren't we getting affluent!".

He also tells her that he is very frustrated negotiating a television script with London. He says that a trip to America he desperately wants to make, is dependent on the television script being accepted. "Do you know" he finally ends the letter, "I never had a holiday in my life".

Christy liked having his poetry read to him. These were the days before the ready availability of taperecorders. So Dr. Sheehan went to Peter Hunt's recording studio in St. Stephen's Green and made a long-playing record of Christy's epic poem called 'The Totempole'. In this way Christy could play it on the gramaphone and listen.

CHAPTER EIGHT

A PAINTING BONANZA : COLLIS' EXILE : A QUESTION OF GOD .

The decision to leave the Clinic did not mean that all the staff there, thought any less of Christy. In early 1957, the Medical Director, Dr. Mary O'Donnell, a gentle Kerrywoman, wrote to him about a scheme intended to give employment to disabled artists. She offered to set up a meeting for him with a Captain Feehan, who was the representative of a new Association. Christy accepted her kind offer, writing: "Please forgive me for having taken such a lengthy time replying to your letter. The fact is, I have only now begun to use my machine again, as it broke down and had to be extensively repaired...I didn't feel quite in the mood to dictate, owing to a persistent sore throat...I wish to say that I should like to accept your kind suggestion that I meet the representative of the Painting Association, next Monday as you say, at home, because I doubt if I could get down to the Clinic owing to the fact that I have to meet some people from Radio Eireann on that afternoon. I trust you know what way to get to Stannaway Road!".

Within a few days Christy was informing Dr. Sheehan of the meeting, surmising on who could be behind such an apparently financially rewarding scheme, as this purported to be. He wrote: "I suppose you have heard that I may be joining this new Association for disabled artists? I had an interesting interview on Monday with the Irish agent, and he gave me a fortnight to make up my mind. In view of the fantastic financial attraction they're offering it may seem rather priggish that there should be any 'making up of mind' at all! Ordinarily, I'd jump at the chance of earning such money, but you see if I accept, it will mean that I will have to, more or less, abandon my writing, or at any rate, treat it as a mere sideline to my painting. That is something I will find it very, very hard to do and just now I cannot contemplate it. I like painting, yes, but I love writing infinitely more. I had never imagined making money by painting, and certainly I never regarded it as a means of making a livelihood. My entire mind was taken up with writing, with carving out a career as a reasonably good author. I built up and canalised all my energy and endeavours towards the fulfilment of such an aim, and it will need a tremendous amount of readjustment to divert that creative force into another channel".

He admitted that he knew that with proper training he could never be more than an average painter, but he had his heart set on becoming a rather good writer and poet. He wrote: "I love writing and want to succeed as a writer. With me writing is not only a passion - it is a necessity, as vital to my nature as the presence of beauty itself and the pursuit of beauty. It can never become secondary to any other interest or calling. I really feel it was the only thing I was made for, and certainly the only thing that affords me the greatest means of self-expression and self-knowledge".

But Christy also possessed a commonsense, which always appeared where the acquisition of money was concerned. He added : " I dare say there would be no sense in turning down the offer absolutely, however, and I will probably give it a trial period of a year or so. The salary sounds incredible and fantastic - £100 per month, plus a percentage on the sale of each picture and its subsequent reproductions. That amounts to about £1,200 or so per annum. Absolutely colossal, isn't it? It all seems to be perfectly genuine and above board, however, which makes the whole business even more intriguing. It is probably run by a couple of eccentric millionaires with uncontrollable philanthropic leanings, who dodder about their gardens all day planting bulbs and cultivating geraniums with a view to extracting nuclear energy from them! Very admirable lunatics, though".

Christy added a footnote about the Clinic: "My Clinic days are now a very dim and unreal part of the past. Dr. O'Donnell told me a new school was being built in the grounds. I wonder will it be used as a school, or for the tortuous gyrations of the physiotherapists?".

Christy had prevailed on Dr. Sheehan, much to the discomfort of the management of the Clinic, to continue giving him speech therapy at his own home. She then began visiting Browns' on a regular basis getting to know all the family intimately, particularly Mrs Brown, or 'Ma Brown', as she called her.

* * * * * *

Another event occurred at this time which probably had some influence on Christy's decision to abandon the Clinic at Sandymount. To explain this, it is necessary to again concentrate briefly on the life of Robert Collis. Collis saw his family as Anglo-Irish. In the 1940s he admired the stand of Churchill and the English after the fall of France. He wrote in his Autobiography, which appears to be in conflict with sentiments expressed in his Carmichael Prize Essay quoted earlier, that he also understood and admired the position of DeValera who was able to steer Ireland along an officially neutral path, while backing the Allies in practical ways, and also allowing Irish citizens who wished to volunteer to join the Allied cause either by conviction or 'simply through the love of adventure'[1].

At the end of the war in 1945, Collis along with a colleague from the Rotunda, Dr. Patrick McClancy, got three months leave from April to August to join a Red Cross mission going to the continent. As such, they were among the first group to relieve the Belsen concentration camp. There he met and fell in love with a Dutch nurse, named Han Hogerzeil. Together they saw shocking scenes of human deprivation. Typical of Collis, he was not content to do his duty, but felt he had to bring a group of Jewish children back to Ireland with him and adopt some of them. He organised the establishment of an open air hospital in Howth called Fairy Hill, to receive the children. Arthur Cox was among the hospital's benefactors.

Back home in Dublin with his wife Phyllis and two teenage boys, Collis told his wife about Han. Phyllis hoped that it had been a wartime romance which he would outgrow. This did not happen. Some years later in London, Han told Collis that she was pregnant. He arranged that she go to live with friends of his in Limerick, and have the baby in Cork. Mother and baby nearly died at the birth, with a Professor of Obstetrics saving Han and Collis saving their baby, Sean. As soon as mother and child were able to travel, Collis sent them to stay in England with his good friends, Cecil Day-Lewis and his wife Jill Balcon. Later they stayed with Collis' brother Jack, and his wife Eirene outside London.

Collis loved Han and Sean and wished them to form a family. He wanted to end living a double life. He realised that to do this would mean him leaving Ireland, Phyllis, and his two sons, who were then of university age. Some years earlier at the Rotunda, he had made friends with a Nigerian doctor, who always wanted him to go to Nigeria and initiate paediatrics there. At this time Collis again met this doctor in London, who introduced him to Abubakar Tafewa Balewa, a Northern Minister in the new Nigerian Administration and a future Prime Minister of the Nigerian Federation.

Within six months of this meeting, Collis had parted from his family in Dublin, saw Han briefly in London and travelled to Ibadan to become Director of a new Paediatric Department at the university for the commencement of the academic year of 1957. He had not notified the Board of the Cerebral Palsy Association of his departure and it was uncertain of his intentions for quite some time. Eventually the Association replaced him on the Board. He did not resign from any of his other appointments least the Nigerian experiment founder. He got leave of absence from his post at the Rotunda. Despite his ground-breaking work there over the years, the hospital authorities were only too happy to facilitate his transfer to Africa. In a publication marking the bi-centenary of that hospital, despite the fulsome and extensive recognition of Collis' historic role, there is also contained some references to another other side of the great man. It reads, "Collis' time in Dublin was to some extent an uneasy one. He was that most dangerous of being, 'a man of ideas', and in their expression and execution was not always tactful"[2]. It also states, "Dr. Collis was a dynamic Director of the Rotunda paediatric service and achieved much. He clearly found it difficult to work with the authority of a Master, and he in turn was not very popular with his obstetric colleagues. Dr. Collis did not mince his words..."[3]. This picture is echoed by Dr. Sheehan in Christopher Fitz-Simon's book "The Boys", about the way Collis functioned at the Cerebral Palsy Association. She is quoted," he bulldozed his way through everything. Before a committee meeting you would be summoned to his rooms in Fitzwilliam Square and every item would be gone through, so that he was completely briefed".

After two years in Nigeria, as Collis has written, "Phyllis with great generosity made it possible for me to marry Han, recognise Sean and bring them both out to Africa"[4]. By that time Han had also become a doctor and was subsequently able to do medical work in Nigeria as Collis became immersed in the medical world of the newly emerging country. Later they had a second baby, Niall, who was born prematurely: 'a poor little handicapped baby'[5], as his father recalled. At the age of eighteen months Collis described Niall as 'a lovely baby with fair waving hair'[6].

* * * * * *

The departure of Robert Collis to Nigeria was somewhat embarrassing for his friends and colleagues. It was especially so for his wife of many years. Christy knew her well and though very sympathetic to her, was unsure of what to say to her in the circumstances. She often corresponded with him and he replied in his long rambling style. In one such letter about a year after the departure of Robert Collis, he reminisces about a literary party held in the Collis household, giving a particularly interesting picture of a poetical recital, which would appear to have been by Richard Murphy:

54 Stannaway Road
Sept. 12th, 1958.

Dear Mrs Collis,

Please do forgive me for taking so long to reply to your charming letter, which I was delighted to receive. My old machine has not been on her best behaviour lately...but I'll have to grin and bear it until I earn enough to purchase one of those machines...of the atomic age !

I was really glad to get your letter, even though it contained the sad news of Robbie's (Collis' son) departure. I was looking forward to seeing him before he left, for only a few weeks before that I had a note from him telling me of the final successes both he and Ivy had gained in their examinations, and promising to drop out to see me sometime. I knew of course that they intended to go away, but had no idea that it was to be so soon. But then of course neither had they! ...Robbie is a fine chap, one of the nicest men I have known... I shall miss him a good deal, for although his time was so taken up with his studies, we were great old pals and I always enjoyed it when we got together and proceeded to get a little 'jarred'! I'll never forget that terribly intellectual party the Doctor gave some time ago, at which there were such glittering stars of the literary firmament as Sean O'Faolain, W.R.Rodgers, Francis MacManus and others, and our artist friend Sean O'Sullivan, who drank nothing but orange that night to the astonishment of us all. A little 'out of it' with all the nabobs, Rob took me aside in a corner, away from the madding crowd, took possession of a large stone jug of some delectable but highly explosive concoction, and quietly, methodically set out to lift me on to a higher plane of consciousness. Unhampered by the fact that his foot was broken and in plaster of Paris at the time, he succeeded very well in his noble task. So well, in fact, that I later 'boned' Mr. O Faolain and proceeded to expound my own literary ideas to him with such heat that without quite realising it, I found myself having an eloquent dialogue with the wall, and looking around to explain this strange state of affairs, saw the said eminent author away at the other end of the room talking rather guardedly to the Doctor and looking covertly across at my semi-recumbent figure on the sofa...

Another cherished recollection remaining to me of that night was that of Robbie hobbling around on his one good foot with the indispensable jug in his hand, replenished early and often from under the Napoleonic nose and slightly reproving eye of his Father! We were both in a very advantageous position that night, Robbie and I, for with him on his broken foot and me with my cerebral palsy, no one could make up their minds whether it was the drink that made us wobbly or our respective bodily disabilities! No one, that is, until I passed out serenely and lay hunched up on the sofa while the doctor and my frantic younger brother - who had come to drive me home - tried in vain to wake me,, until finally the doc threw me over his capable shoulder and lugged me downstairs and into the car! I was relieved to hear the next day that by that time all the intellectuals had departed, so that no one witnessed my ignoble exit but dear Rusty, and I was sure that he wouldn't breathe a word of it to anyone. I had a rather faint remembrance also of endeavouring to flirt with what I took to be a rather pretty Indian girl, but when I asked the Doctor the next day who it was, he informed me with a huge grin that it was no other than Ivy! Was my face Red!!

I also remember an English poet called Murphy, a bit paradoxical in itself, who came, a tall, saturnine, desperately thin young man, carrying a baby in a Moses basket, and his very self-possessed wife, who was carrying nothing but her handbag and who seemed to accept this reversal of marital procedure as being as it should be. Poor Murphy had a difficult time of it, trying to recite his newest verse and holding tightly on to his progeny in the basket; it all turned out fine eventually when he got a little tight and plucked up sufficient hardihood to deposit the basket on the floor at his feet and declaim his poetry to his heart's content. I thought he looked somewhat like Lazarus risen from the dead. His wife looked like Cleopatra at a loose end, brooding about Antony. It was, all in all, a gorgeous party up to the time of my total eclipse.

I have good news about the art project. I had a visit from Capt. Feehan the Irish agent for the Association...I have often tried to work according to a determined formula, for it is a bad thing to be enslaved by one's imagination any time it chooses to exercise itself. But it was never a success...There are times when I cannot even bear to look at my typewriter or a sheet of unspoilt paper, and this apathetic mood might last for days, even weeks; then there are other times when absolutely nothing has any real existence for me but whatever I may be writing at the time. I am subject to both maladies; complete indifference, or at any rate a gnawing discontent, and then a sudden and irresistible passion for writing and nothing else, so that for nights and days on and on I go without sleep and am nothing but a slave to a capricious imagination. What stands to me, I suppose, is my great capacity for food and drink even during those mental aberrations, for as they say in Dublin, I'm a terrible man for me gut !!!

Thank God, things on the home front are beginning to improve somewhat, though still slowly. I suppose it's a chronic condition at 54, this eternal depression. We all eat too much I daresay, without having always the 'wherewithal' to get the commodities. There isn't anything very constructive that I can do now, unless I come up with another best seller! I am grateful my Mother is well and quite unbroken, the brothers have all gone back to England after the holidays with the usual promises of support, and my sisters keep on producing babies with pious regularity almost every year, perhaps in an unconscious effort to emulate Mother! Until I hear from you again, goodbye, take care of yourself and thanks for everything. Chris. .

Though Robert Collis' sojourn in Nigeria would last for up to fourteen years, it did not mean that his connection with Christy Brown was terminated. Collis was extremely successful in Nigeria. He continued to summer in Ireland and undertake much international travel connected with his work.

Christy joined the new Disabled Artists Association and commenced training. His painting style changed dramatically. He began to go in for heavy outlines and dark shadows. His work was unusually sombre, full of sadness. He did a lot of suffering Heads of the Lord in Crucifixion. At that time he still had a deep religious faith. Early in 1959, he announced to Dr. Sheehan that he was growing a beard. Later he described himself to her as a cross between Hamlet and Christ.

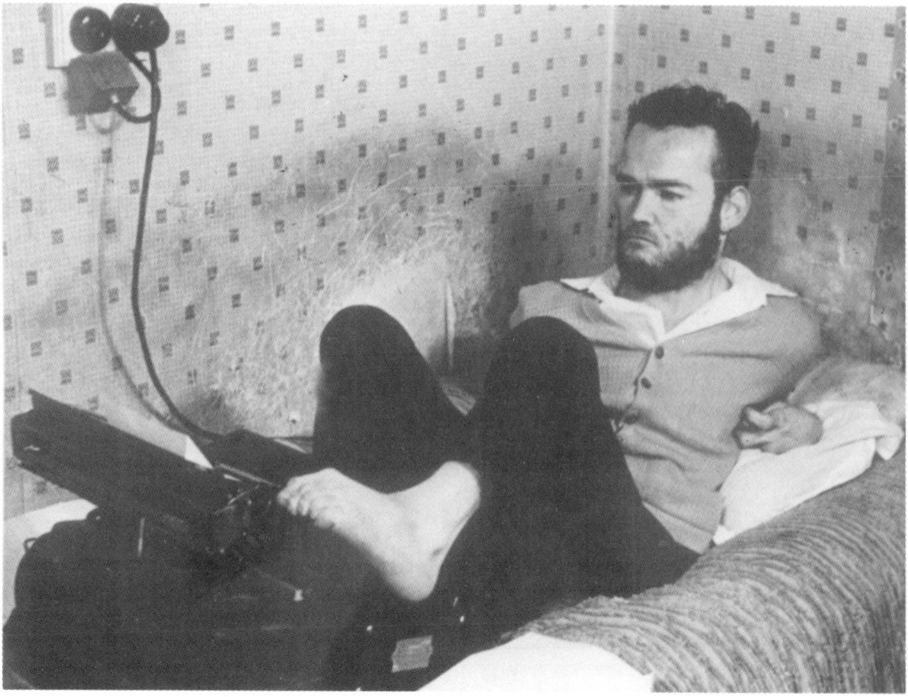

Writer at work.

Dublin was always a bitchy literary city with begrudgery the norm. Christy Brown did not escape this, as rumour held that the real author of 'My Left Foot' was Robert Collis. Brown was well aware of this and broached the subject in another revealing letter to his mentor Dr. Patricia Sheehan, who surprisingly enough, was also among those who believed that Collis must have been the real author. He wrote: “I’ve started writing the sequel to ‘My Left Foot’ - and it is not called ‘My Right Foot’!! This is serious. I began it a fortnight ago and have the first three chapters off to my satisfaction. The publishers of my first book have often inquired when the second one was coming along, but I did not want to start it until I was quite sure I was ready. I do feel so now. As you probably know - though you were always too sweet to hint at it to me - many intelligent people believe it was Collis who really produced that first book, and I was merely a tag. I have met several persons, friends and strangers alike, who hold this quaint opinion, and God bless them, I would not dream of disillusioning them by getting red-faced and outraged and claiming damages for libel, in order to reaffirm my literary paternity. I must make it clear though, that this second book is by no means a mere attempt to humble the unbelievers; I want to write it in the first place because I feel it is time to do so, and also because I want to satisfy my own creative urge. And I feel too that I have something to say, and will say it in the most interesting and entertaining way I can. It will cover the last four years from the publication and reception of my first book up to the present day. I plan to write it in the literary style of the other book, but the actual subject matter, the living material of the whole thing will have deeper implications and undercurrents in keeping with the advance and maturity of my adult life.

You see this time it won’t be so much a cripple endeavouring to overcome his handicaps, but rather an adult personality faced with the far more intimidating problem of overcoming himself after his handicaps, his crippledom having ceased to hold the same terrors for him. I know all this sounds involved, but I'm hopeless at discussing and describing my own stuff with anyone else except myself, and particularly in cold print. I can only dash off the damn thing in my own way and leave the criticism and judgement to others. I don’t intend to actually finish the book straight away. My plan is rather a mercenary one. I want to get it to the half way mark, and then see if the publishers are interested enough to finance my trip to America in order to finish the book there. This would give the book greater interest and variety, add vastly to the material, and incidentally fulfil one of my biggest ambitions all at once. I’m afraid this subterfuge - yes? is my only real chance of getting to the USA, while it is still there, before we're all blown to hell by Khrushchev and Co. Where are all my fabulous riches? Gone the way of all flesh, though they weren't exactly as fabulous as some people seemed to imagine. I’m not complaining though - why should I? I spent not wisely but too well when the ready cash was all too ready, and now my affairs are handled on an evertightening string. That’s life! As the song says, it's all in the game! I'm ashamed to admit to such weakness, but I'd do the same again and enjoy it as much. Just now I'm lucky to have a few pints at the weekend, let alone champagne and caviar! (Which of course I've never tasted)". Christy then spoke about his relationship with the Clinic and his abandonment of therapy there. He knew he would have to deal with it in his book and he wanted to enlist Dr. Sheehan's help in the matter. He wrote ," You know I had my sincere reasons for leaving and I want to put them down in as fair and honest a manner as possible. I cannot possibly omit this, being as it was one of the most difficult and unpleasant decisions I have had to make. I believe if I put it all down honestly and sincerely, exactly as it seemed to me at the time, I cannot offend or step on anyone's toes".

Christy also mentioned another potentially thorny matter. He had read several times in the paper how the Clinic was fundraising for their new buildings. But he had not made any contribution. He imagines some of the comments that might be made about him at Sandymount; "Still no endowment from that Brown creature...disgusting ingratitude...shameless profligate...lousy bastard...". He adds, "Ah well, my beard won't go grey overnight I trust!". Even in later times when he was again in a position to have made a donation to the Clinic fundraising campaigns, he never did so. This was no doubt probably a natural inclination to cut adrift completely from a time and a place where he was very dependent. But it was also due to his disaffection with the establishment there and its treatment of staff with whom he had established close relations, particularly his mentor Dr. Sheehan.

By agreeing to give him speech therapy after he had abandoned the Clinic, she gradually became persona non grata at Sandymount and eventually resigned her position there. Dr. Sheehan remembers her days of going to visit the Browns : "When I used to go over to Kimmage to visit Christy, Bobby my husband would drive me over. Then Bobby and Ma Brown would chat in the kitchen, while I went out to Christy's study in the yard. Sometimes he would just want me to talk, or for me to read his poetry to him. Other times he just wanted reassurance that I was still around and 'cared'. Then after a while the 'game' would begin... How long could he keep my concentration and keep me away from Bobby, not in any spiteful way, but rather as a boost to his morale, to show that I was still interested in him, and that he could hold me... not in a physical way, but by his personality, spirit and magnetism. The longer he could hold me the more chuffed his ego. The game was harmless; in fact I don't think I ever caused Christy a lustful thought".

Dr. Sheehan recalls one fundraising event for the Clinic held in the Shelbourne Ballroom. Brendan Behan and John B. Keane were two of the celebrities present. Christy's comment to her about how each of then would write of a character looking for a drink in a pub went; "Keane's character would say 'with your long arm and your strong arm would you be pouring me a glass of solid stout Paidin Beag', while Behan's would say, 'Jaysus, I'm gasping' ". Ann Jones said of Dr. Sheehan; "She was coming to our house since I was a child. She was a great friend of my Mammy's. She used to spend hours out in the study talking to Christy. Then she'd often go out with my Mam. She was a great friend all her life to the lot of us".

Christy's health was generally excellent, making the point that people with a disability are not 'sick' and should not be treated as such in an overtly hospital type environment. But shortly after the last letter he wrote to Dr. Sheehan, he got seriously ill and went through an extremely difficult period of an almost 'long night's journey of the soul'. He got a bad dose of the 'flu and seemed to have recovered. He went back to work and simply collapsed. He had overworked and overdrank for the previous few months and "had to pay the price for my zeal in both capacities".

He had to go to a Nursing Home for a month. His soul became tortured as he pondered on the meaning of his life, on God, and on being a disabled man. In May of 1959 he wrote to Dr. Sheehan: "I suppose really the reason for my downfall in health was more emotional than physical. Lately I have been invaded by hopelessly conflicting emotions and thoughts, and I seem to be as well acquainted with myself as I like to think in moments of smug self-assurance and satisfaction. I often have the childish notion that God is in the wrong place, that He is on the wrong side of the celestial fence, and that the more we strive to reach him the more He repulses us. Five centuries ago I would have been branded a heretic for holding such a view...today heresy is a vital part of our society, though we know it variously as democracy, free thinking, and just plain genius. Not that I am overwhelmed by the desire to attain piety; I wish merely to be sure of my beliefs, and to know how to read the sign-posts along the way. In every man's life the question of God must inevitable arise, and of his own individual relationship with Him, and when it does arise, it is inevitably of supreme importance. I shudder at times to think that this hourly-decaying flesh should, perhaps after all, be all that we have to live for, that we hold in our little mechanism of a body the sum-total of all we were, and are, and ever will be, and that with the destruction of that body the meaning and value of our existence will die out too. Is that not a horrifying thought, a ghastly speculation? Yet it is the essence of all the unrest, uncertainty and near despair which has settled almost palpably upon me lately. I know it is also the essence of the world's despair, and that men have had this very same fear since they began to be men and not mere brutes; for each one of us however, it comes as a fearful new experience, and with a terrifying significance suited to our individual natures and the circumstances of our lives. The more I am driven away from people the more I am driven away into myself, the more I must seek to find answers to the most important questions about myself, the more I must try to find God in some unknown part of me. I think of Van Gogh's terrible saying, 'he that loves God cannot expect to be loved by God in return'. There seems to be a grain of some awful truth in that. Our virtue seems to be an excuse to be sanctimonious and hypocritical, and we are consumed with vulgar piety and petty righteousness. I do not visualise an entirely amoral world, nor even an honest-to-goodness immoral one, but it seems to me there is an intolerable absence of free air and space in our modern religious code. This, however, does not worry me as much as my own reflections upon life. Religion is the overcoat for the masses; we must people the sanctuary of our own dark little souls with our own images, and forge out of our experience a philosophy that will lead us to where we want to go. I suppose you might call my unhappiness 'cosmic', and dismiss it as such, but that is no use; it is only sacrificing the apple for the appletree, the ripple for the ocean, one human heart for all the human hearts in the world. This mood of intense speculation will no doubt pass as all things pass, but that isn't the answer, is it?

It is while we are experiencing life that we must think and probe and search in ourselves if we are to understand anything of it at all. Each fact helps us to build a conviction, each conviction helps us to build a faith, and faith is the only thing that gives human life any meaning or value.

If I had more time for reading, perhaps I should find answers to some of the questions, but I become restless and unsure when I examine the fruits of the minds of other men, and am left with the selfish thought that I am neglecting my own. While I was unwell and in harness, I turned to reading St. Augustine and 'The Confessions', from which I derived much consolation; I also explored Thomas Mann and found delight in the clarity and preciseness of his thought, and comfort in the largeness of his heart. But I am alone still in my search for some workable code of living. You will appreciate from your experience that this matter of having faith and meaning is of far greater importance to people like myself, than it is to the physically normal person. When you are created so that ordinary contact with the world is strictly limited, you are necessarily thrown upon your own company and if you happen at all to be the sensitive type, then the isolation and solitude will make you intensely attuned to life and all the currents and undercurrents, like a weed played upon by the wind.

Do you call all this just morbid introspection? That may well be, but it is surely beside the point? We do not change things by giving them names; and the least that can be said of any of us in the final analysis, is that we tried to know ourselves, and to live with that knowledge.

I am sorry for heaping my miseries upon your very attractive head; do forgive me. I do sometimes let the mask slip. Give my regards to whatever remaining friends I may still have at the clinic, and tell them I'm enjoying disgustingly vigourous health".

A troubled Christy.

CHAPTER NINE

FR. CLEARY : A PASSPORT TO AMERICA : BETH MOORE : ALCOHOLIC CELTIC TWILIGHT.

The USA had been one of Christy's targets for some time. He had been corresponding since 1955 with a lady who, on reading his first book, wrote to him full of praise and gratitude for the hope he gave to other disabled people. Her name was Beth Moore and she lived with her husband in Stamford, Connecticut. She was involved in rehabilitation work in a voluntary capacity, but also had a keen interest in English literature. Beth had met Collis on one of his earlier American tours and he had told her about his protege. Through the Cerebral Palsy Association of Connecticut, she invited Christy to spend a summer at her home. Collis had told Christy that Beth could be a great help to him in his writing endeavours.

In 1960 a transatlantic trip was still something of a marathon journey for an able bodied person. Christy knew that he would need a minder, if he was to make the trip. Luckily for him, Robert Collis was back from Nigeria for the summer and going to America, on another lecture tour. He offered to escort Christy across the Atlantic on the fifteen hour journey.

Fr. Michael Cleary was a curate in St. Bernadette's Church Clogher Road, the parish the Browns lived in. At that time Americans came to Ireland with a view to adopting Irish children. Fr. Cleary used to take the visiting Americans to see Christy painting, in his early days, thereby supplementing the family income. As happened with so many people he encountered, Fr. Cleary was to remain a life-long friend of the Browns, being available to help whenever he was called upon. A visa was required to enter the USA, so Christy made application to the American Embassy in Dublin. Fr. Cleary later called to the Embassy, expecting to collect the visa for Christy. The lady consul had never heard of Christy Brown and insisted that he would have to appear in person to transact the business. The Consul's office was at the end of a long garden in an old coach-house, at the rear of the Embassy in Merrion Square. Fr. Cleary had to half push, half lift his companion along the path to be interviewed by the officious lady. With legs, arms and head flailing, for great effect, Christy instructed Fr. Cleary to remove the shoe and sock from his left foot. Then he casually asked the consul, what exactly she wished him to sign.[1]

In later years Mary Brown, Christy's widow, in commenting on this passport, wrote to me:

"As you can see from the passport photograph, Christy altered a lot. He was rather influenced by American crew cuts and shirts at the time. By the way they have his height at 4' 2", which is farcical, because they just guessed it (as he was sitting in his wheelchair). He was in fact 5' 1".

We used to have great crack singing that old song, Four Foot two, Eyes of blue Has anyone seen my boy?".

Christy soon conveyed his first impressions of America to Katriona Maguire. On 1 August 1960, he wrote:

"We arrived in New York at about 08.30 local time, which means we were flying for little over fifteen hours...Betty was there to meet us when we landed at Idlewild. You will understand this was our first actual meeting outside of our letters. She wore an orange dress, and as we came through the Customs gallery she waved to us and lifted her arms above her head in a victory salute. After we dropped Dr. Collis off at his hotel, she took me to see some of the sights of New York...She is the most wonderful person imaginable, humorous, gay, thoughtful, practical when it comes to dealing with me, oh so many things in one!

She has a beautiful home right on the New England coast, with a lovely stretch of privately owned beach where we all had great fun splashing about in the water. The heat is great, but surprisingly I find it not as oppressive as I feared it would be. The clothes I took with me were too heavy, so Beth went out and got me some light things instead. I look a typical 'Yank from Connecticut' in my almost-white trousers and teashirt !

I'm beguiling them here with what Betty calls my Irish brogue, which I never dreamed until now I possessed! The countryside around Stamford and the suburbs of New York are exquisitely beautiful; in aspect almost like that of Co. Wicklow, green and rolling and soft, with glimpses of lake between leafy canopies and long winding roads, with here and there old-style taverns with picturesque signs hanging outside. The houses are fascinating, all wooden structures, some dating back to the sixteenth and seventeenth centuries, all wonderfully quaint and some grand, porticoed in marble with spacious lawns lipping large ponds and balconies rising tier upon tier.

Beth's house has twelve rooms and stands in its own ground, with the beach just a few yards down the road; we had a picnic there the other night, from early evening until the moon was high and the waters were dappled in silver, with the little boats and yachts and sailing skiffs bobbing on the tide. We sang songs and ate hamburgers and hotdogs and drank glasses of Tom Collins' (iced gin and soda) and bottles of Guinness stout (trust me to root out the genuine article !).

We're going to Stratford next week with Dr. Collis to see 'Antony and Cleopatra' with Katherine Hepburn. I've been interviewed and photographed by the press several times since I arrived, and the story has been in several papers. I'm frightened by the speed and ingenuity of how they do things over here, but am determined to seem quite casual and matter-of-fact about it all...some of them have pretty queer ideas about Ireland which I've been busily debunking...they think the only traffic is in bicycles and that we eat nothing but corned beef and cabbage...But believe me, I'm enjoying myself hugely and intend to get the utmost fun out of everything. And in this I have a wholehearted companion in Beth. A grand girl. I do miss home and all the clan, and especially the cobbly old streets of Dublin, and the pubs. Still, this is my holiday and the chance of a lifetime, and I'm taking it with both hands, or feet?".

The Americans suited Christy. Their attitude was, if he had a problem, they had a solution. As is clear from his letter to Katriona, he had become very close to his hostess. The whole experience uplifted him. It was only after he returned home in October that he again wrote to Katriona and expressed vividly and courageously how meeting Beth, in the flesh, had gone. Clearly, Christy had added substantially and crucially to the women in his life.

"...The first few days were spent in getting used to the surroundings and getting to know Beth's family.[She had four children](Author's note). It was a completely new world to me, needing a complete reorientation of thought and attitude. I was at last completely removed from the Brown circle of existence, absolutely 'on my own', with whole new problems to face that were both physical and emotional. Beth and I had shared five astonishing years of intense and candid correspondence and had in that time come to know and understand the peculiar nature and mould of each other's character with a knowledge that in some aspects went deeper than 'actual', or physical experience and encounter. But here we were now, face to face, in the midst of reality, stripped of all the automatic and unconscious escape-mechanisms and subterfuges which, inevitably, one construes in the world of letter-writing. I had travelled 3,000 miles to test a dream, an ideal, and to face a challenge. I feared the ideal would be less idealistic, the dream less than perfect than what I had known through the letters. And they were. And I was at first confused and frightened and alarmed, until I attained the power and courage to accept the change. And with acceptance was born a wonderful sense of thanks-giving and relief and, ultimately, of sheer joy and happiness. If it was less than perfect, less idealistic, it was only because my hopes and needs and longings were no longer wrapped in dreams, but were transformed at last into realities and the reality is always less perfect than the dreams, until you accept the fact and then the reality assumes a sweetness and vividness of its own, a keen, moving and fluctuating life that was before unknown and impossible in your dream-world of perfect living and love. You threw off the shining cloak of dreams, and put on the plain cloak of reality, and if at first the coat was rather threadbare, the eternal and ever-changing woof of life sewed many fine and intricate patterns and colours through the otherwise sombre material...".

Mona Byrne remembers Christy returning home with all his new American gear, especially the velcro, which gave him such independence. At home, the sense of euphoria lasted for a short time and thereafter he plunged into the depths of despair. Within a few months, in February 1961, he wrote to Dr. Sheehan, who performed a different role for him than Katriona :

"Dear Dr. Pat,

No doubt you'll be somewhat surprised to hear from me. I just now realised we were perilously close to losing contact completely, and decided I'd better write and reestablish the feud - I mean friendship - which for me has been such a happy one. Indeed I don't know if you're still remotely interested in hearing from me again, but that's a risk I must face. And bravely I face it.

How are you? I reflect it must be almost two years since I last saw you, which seems incredible. It mightn't be so long, but it certainly feels so. I had a visit from Katriona Maguire recently...I trust your husband is well and in the pink. (Mostly I don't inquire after husbands, but he's such a nice guy.) How is Sandymount really? Is it still staffed by decrepit old ladies on loan from the Rheumatism Clinic? (With one obvious exception of course). Has the new wing opened yet? I've been out of contact with that part of my life for so long I hardly know what questions to ask. I often see the ambulance whizzing past, crowded as always, but with different faces; and would you believe it, a feeling of nostalgia sometimes comes upon me, though it never lasts very long...

Well, as you probably know by now, I've seen the New World in all its sometimes artificial - glory, came home, and been hungering ever since to go back, which I will do just as soon as I earn enough money...

I travelled with Collis, who had returned from Nigeria a week before. He left me in New York and went on a marathon lecture tour which took him to Washington, Kentucky and Missouri, among other places and during which he earned himself a sizeable quantity of dollars - more power to his elbow. I stayed in Stamford Connecticut, throughout my stay, with my friend Betty Moore and her family, in a delightful house on the coast with a private beach attached and Long Island Sound almost at the doorstep.

The trip itself, in its purely therapeutic perspective, was an object lesson in self-aid and enlightenment. In many ways it was the most wonderful experience of my life. I learned so much about myself that I had never known or suspected before...I was fearfully hesitant and uninitiated the first few days - I kept thinking, 'My God, three thousand miles away and absolutely alone with people I never met before; 'Awful! Physically I had never been so completely dependent on my own resources, and the prospect of spending almost two months in this state was unnerving. Then the panic ceased, my insecurity subsided, and somewhat to my own amazement and certainly to Betty's , I there and then proceeded to outdo the Americans...I did things I had never done before or thought I could do - I went swimming every day - with the help of an inflated rubber tube and closely watched by Beth, herself an excellent swimmer; I bathed entirely without aid, dressed and undressed, which was made easy since the Americans wear so little in the Summer; I learned to drink through polythene straws, iced tea and canned beer and, inevitably, Irish whiskey; I went to a luncheon given for me by the Cerebral Palsy Association held in the Catskill Mountains in a ranch; I went to the United Nations, had a specially conducted tour conducted by a luscious girl guide from Tennessee, and dined in the delegates dining hall...I went to the top of the Empire State - indescribable, and took the famous ferryboat trip round Manhattan Island...

We drove down to see Sheila in Boston and spent a weekend there; do you remember Sheila?... She's older now than when I first wrote fervently idealistic poetry about her, but so are we all, and she is still as charming, lovable and lovely as ever in my prejudiced eyes.

I went to moonlight barbecue parties held down on the beach, where everyone sang in turn their favourite folk song in between the bourbon and the rye, and ate enormous steaks and hot dogs and pizza pies and lit their own separate bonfires by scooping out hollows in the sand and stacking them with twigs and branches and anything inflammable...when it came my turn I gave them 'The Sally Gardens', or perhaps it would be something more fiery like 'Kevin Barry'...those evenings were unforgettable... and the frank friendly faces of the people around me lit by the flames from the spiralling bonfires - one among them that meant something deep and beautiful to me...".

Christy would have enjoyed writing and reliving those experiences, especially his declaration of love for his hostess. He then came to the real purpose of his letter to Dr. Sheehan, to whom he did not mind exposing his hurt and grief. He continued :

"Well, it all seems very long ago now, and perhaps it is somewhat superfluous talking about it..I was faced with a terrible sense of frustration and depression the first few weeks after my return - it was like coming down from the mountain to level ground again, an awful doubled awareness of the narrowness and isolation of my life in Kimmage; I'd say it was like re-entering a prison cell after one glorious spell of freedom in the broad world outside, only that sounds too corny and hackneyed. I lost interest in my 'work' as I like to call it, found fault with my family and friends, and took badly to drink -five out of seven days each week found me in an alcoholic Celtic twilight, with no appetite for thought or activity. In short, I must have become pretty impossible to live with, and how the hell my mother put up with me remains one of the miracles of the age. Oh, not that I was physically violent or obstreperous...Most times I just sat brooding in my study with a whiskey bottle at my elbow, burdened with a sense of loss and disillusion that was almost physical in intensity. But it was this very attitude, I see now, which was the cruellest blow to my poor Mother's efforts to understand and placate me. I felt somehow that Kimmage was trying to absorb me once more, to reassimilate and immerse me in the old and too painfully familiar vortex of daily monotony and sameness, to anaesthetize my brain and dull its perceptions of a higher perspective of living and doing...".

Christy often contemplated suicide, though he was not obsessive or morbid about it, believing that such thoughts were inevitable for anyone scarred by life. But he always concluded that he did enjoy living. He was a tough character and his Mother would not allow him to destroy himself. Nevertheless the aftermath of his trauma had forced him to spend a two month period in hospital. He did improve, otherwise he would have been unable to write this honest and hopeful letter. He went on:

"I am emerging from my depression-ridden hibernation, breaking out of my glass castle...While there is life there is no choice but to accept it and live it to the best of one's abilities, and anyway it is extremely hard to live hating oneself day by day. One is oddly attached to oneself, somehow or other! So I have come round to thinking...It is entirely up to myself if I am to remain incarcerated here in Kimmage indefinitely, or if I am to break away and begin an independent and creatively useful life of my own. Reading over this, it might strike an outsider as rather a priggish thing to say, but I think you know what I mean...As to the more salient question of whether I will ever get married or continue to live in my present state of celibate bachelorhood...that must remain in the inscrutable stars! Not that I haven't met 'the right one'...trouble is, as always, somebody else met her before me!! And so it goes.

My Mother is well and in good spirits despite all her worries - unemployment, negligent sons and daughters across Channel, indolent sons and daughters here - the woman really is a blooming miracle. Dr. Collis has been presented with a brand new son by his second wife Han, in Ibadan, and the beloved physician himself has gone on a lecture tour of India in his usual forgetful and unhampered fashion...I don't know how or where the first Mrs Collis is now...I feel so damn sorry for her, even if...It would have taxed a woman of far greater spirit than she to live with Bob Collis...But he remains an astonishing man.

And here's hoping I will be forgiven and condoned once more!".

Later that same year, Christy sent a poem to Katriona Maguire, without indicating clearly who the subject was :

" INDIFELITY "

Deaths' strong hand shall clasp me long before I tire
Of watching you, and cast me all suddenly
Into the black loneliness and mire
Of the last land. There, waiting patiently.
One timeless day I'll feel a soft wind blowing
Through the wilderness, see a slow star
move across the tide,
Hear about me the stir of the ancient dead,
unknowing - And trembling,
I shall know that you have died.

I shall watch you come, a white and smiling dream,
Tread lightly through the dim unanswering host,
Stop, and vaguely search, and like a gleam
Pass by unseeing my poor bewildered ghost.
And you shall toss your brown delightful head,
And laugh, and flirt, and forget that you are dead!!

1961.

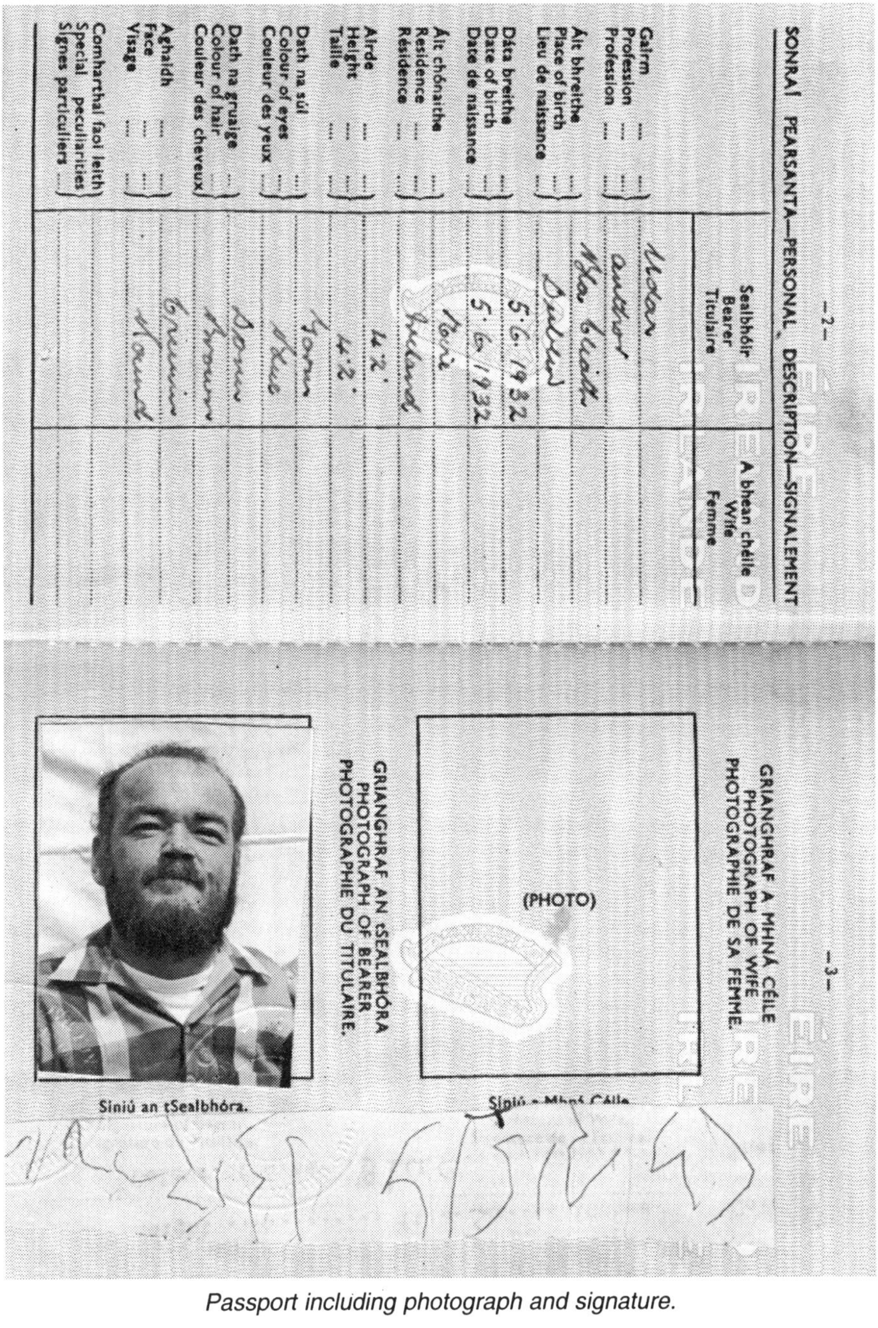

– 2 –

SONRAÍ PEARSANTA—PERSONAL DESCRIPTION—SIGNALEMENT

	Sealbhóir / Bearer / Titulaire	A bhean chéile / Wife / Femme
Gairm / Profession / Profession		
Áit bhreithe / Place of birth / Lieu de naissance		
Dáta breithe / Date of birth / Date de naissance		
Áit chónaithe / Residence / Résidence		
Airde / Height / Taille		
Dath na súl / Colour of eyes / Couleur des yeux		
Dath na gruaige / Colour of hair / Couleur des cheveux		
Aghaidh / Face / Visage		
Comharthaí faoi leith / Special peculiarities / Signes particuliers		

– 3 –

GRIANGHRAF A MHNÁ CÉILE
PHOTOGRAPH OF WIFE
PHOTOGRAPHIE DE SA FEMME.

(PHOTO)

GRIANGHRAF AN tSEALBHÓRA
PHOTOGRAPH OF BEARER
PHOTOGRAPHIE DU TITULAIRE.

Síniú an tSealbhóra.

Síniú a Mhná Céile

Passport including photograph and signature.

CHAPTER TEN

ROMANTIC FANTASIES OF PEOPLE WITH DISABILITY: WITHOUT WINGS OR VOICE : RADHARC.

The succeeding years were difficult ones for Christy. His mother's health was deteriorating. She had an ulcer, heart and blood pressure problems. She continued to work, leaving the house at six oclock in the morning to clean offices. She needed the money. She worried about Christy who, apart from a younger brother, was the only one left at home.

Drink continued to be a major part of Christy's life. One particular public house hit on a novel way of seeking to attract customers. It provided free drink to Christy and Brendan Behan, whose presence it was thought, would draw in the public.

Sometimes, Mrs Brown, who was not averse to a drink, would join them. Christy liked to observe people getting drunk, because their speech got slurred and became worse than his own. He relaxed after a few drinks and his speech improved consequently, as he stopped putting so much effort into it. On one occasion Christy and his Mother were both removed from a pub, because the management, not knowing Christy, assumed he was drunk. On drinking occasions, Mrs Brown loved to berate the medical profession for having advised her to have had her son institutionalised.

Christy had been writing a play named 'Mrs Brennan', which he hoped to submit to the Abbey Theatre. He held out some hope for it, as Ria Mooney and Ray McNally, two well-known Abbey actors, both expressed interest in his first draft. He was also planning a new book on his mother. He tried to resume painting, realising that it offered his best guarantee of financial security.

Katriona Maguire continued to give Christy great attention, despite starting her own family. She believed that their relationship was always a Platonic one and that she provided stepping stones for him in his development. In return he felt utterly free to reveal his innermost thoughts to her. She said that she always answered his straightforward letters to her. Though they saw a lot of each other, he continued to write to her regularly. She did not enter into his philosophical arguments, finding his developing intellect, awesome. But she loved his company and enjoyed his poetry which he continually sent to her. In March of 1962 he wrote to her, first apologising for the bad typing:

"which isn't my fault but the machine, or 'Iron Sally', as I call her, which is going down the glen hard and fast. This typewriter is fifteen years old and is more or less a museum piece today, but as the new model costs £200 at the least, it looks as if I'll have a series of nervous breakdowns before I'll be able to buy a new one, unless I become a new Picasso or Brendan Behan overnight, which is extremely unlikely as I don't happen to particularly admire either.

It was the loveliest surprise to see you on Tuesday morning, and the drive was beautiful - also the driver. Yes indeed, as you remarked, one could well be in Switzerland or Austria up there around Glencree and Glencullen; it was a white-and-blue world, the sun a great crystal jewel hanging in the sky, with the burnished terrace of copper-tinted pine trees fading away into the dazzling distance and the mountains lilting behind like giants with white woollen nightcaps. It was so strange to think that barely a half an hour before, I was sitting in my stuffy little backroom with a smelly parafin heater, worrying about a play, and then there I was not long afterwards, sitting on a log-bench looking down upon the city, you just a few yards away laughing at the antics of your young son and his friends, and looking almost as young as the morning itself and just as lovely. I must try and write a poem about it, don't you think? I hope you forgive my romantic nature; it is something I was born with and cannot help.

A girl once told me, a very beautiful girl, that it was dangerous for people in my position to indulge in romantic fantasies. I suppose she was being kind and eminently practical, but I have puzzled over her remark ever since and have not been able to discover the truth of it. If people such as I can not be romantic, what the hell can we be - anchorites? As long as we know we are indulging in fantasies, not what is so loosely called 'real life', I do not see why a physical disability should preclude any romance in ones life. Life is the greatest romance of all, not in an abstract way as the scientists and philosophers and anthropologists see it, but as we live it and feel it and respond to it with our minds and hearts and senses. If I happen to be more vulnerable, more susceptible to the challenge of life and love, it is my misfortune or blessing, whichever way I meet the challenge: either way the presence of pain will be inevitable, as a stimulant or a disaster. I will cherish my romantic fantasies as long as I live, knowing them to be as real as anything else in life and more acceptable than the so-called 'realities' of others. Life has made me as 'practical' as the next person, but it has never robbed me of my dreams and I am as much an idealist now as I was in the old days, hurting just as deeply even if the pain does not last very long and I am better equipped mentally and emotionally to deal with it. I could no more not be romantic than I could fly to the moon; without this romantic streak, I would be even duller and less original than I am. If my kind of particular artistic appreciation lies with beautiful women...who the hell is complaining? Dante wasn't confined to Beatrice I bet, and it is an irrefutable fact of history that behind every great poem or book or painting, there is a woman - or women, since these fellows were usually accustomed to pluralities".

Katriona realised that this aspect of Christy's personality could make him especially vulnerable to women who took him really serious and responded in the way he wished. He was accustomed to write to any woman who took his fancy. All his friends and family could do, was to hope for the best for him should that situation arise.

In his letter Christy immediately realised that he did not have to argue his cause because Katriona was completely on his side. He confesses that he is being facetious if not irrelevant, adding;

"I feel humble that a girl like you...should find time to spare for someone like myself with so little to recommend me. I rejoice in a friendship that has lasted almost fifteen years and, far from waning, has grown in stature and depth over the years. You have given my life so much richness of thought and feeling, instilled into it a certainty of purpose and provided it with an anchor at a time when it drifted without course and in a vacuum. It would be so easy for me to be merely grateful to you, but my nature is not placid enough for that; my convictions about life go too deeply for me to experience such a facile emotion as gratitude about something which is so deeply embedded in my life. I was so afraid that you would misunderstand and feel uncomfortable, so afraid that in fact that you would stop coming to see me, that it was really most heroic of me to try and even describe my feelings to you; and indeed the word 'emotion' is quite wrong, for it has a certain air of inconstancy and brevity about it, that is absolutely out of keeping with what is in my mind and heart about you. One can feel emotional about a beautiful sunset or a piece of music, and yet forget them entirely as they die away. One can feel like that with many people too and forget with equal ease. There are so many shades and grades of certainty and certitude about human feeling, so many subliminations and idealisations of human love, that you are terribly open to doubt and suspicion if you should speak too prodigally of 'love'. Yet it is impossibly narrow-minded and crippling to think of love only as centred in one particular person. There is so much to love in life. What a pitiable epitaph to die tomorrow - without ever having loved or been loved...".

Christy then included a poem which his American friend approved of, and whose approval appeared so important to him. He says; "Here is a little poem that Betty liked very much and which I hope you will like too. She says - Beth - that at last I have written a poem which has got something to recommend it technically as well as emotionally, but then she is one of my sternest critics, in more ways than one...Oh Katriona, do you think I will ever be a poet? That is what I want to be more than anything else, for to me life is extraordinarily beautiful, and I want to sing about it, but at times I feel like a bird trapped in a cage without wings or voice".

But I offer not my verse
to the clamorous universe :
I sing to you and you alone.

AFFINITY

We two have found the key
Of treasured joys yet to be:
We have found the hidden way
To the light of sweeter day.
We two can laugh time apart
In the warmth of heart to heart;
We can mock affliction's hand
And wander thro' our secret land.

We two have stood and smiled in the rain
And felt joy in the depth's of pain :
We have felt our maker's lips
On our brows in the night's eclipse.

We two can thread the long white road,
Strong to bear each other's load:
We can fear the yearning roll
Across the miles, from soul to soul.

We two have known the inward gnawing
Of a need slowly dawning:
We have known the soft delight
Of a room flame-lit and quiet.

We two can say a million things
In the silence that sings ;
For we know the beauty and wonder
That no earthly pain can sunder.

In 1962 the Radio Telefis Eireann 'Radharc' production unit decided to make a documentary programme about Christy. He spent much time preparing for the event. 'Radharc' was a religious affairs programme and its producers were three Catholic priests, Frs. Des Forrestal, Joe Dunne and Peter Lemass. Christy found the actual filming very hard work. The regime of takes and retakes did not appeal to him. He found that because of the strain, he was making even more than his normal facial grimaces while talking into microphones. His suggestion that a few stiff whiskeys before filming would help, was not taken seriously. Conscious of a likely opportunity, he had several of his paintings placed strategically so that they would be prominent in the film scenes.

He hoped that this might lead to commissions or purchases. The long wait for the film to be screened on television was difficult for Christy and his family, as they were nervous about the outcome. In the event he was very pleased with the result, commenting that "These young priests certainly know their job". He was very impressed with his Mother in the film, saying "She'd do wonders with one of those Abbey plays if she was put into it! Sarah Allgood's not in it!".

But it was Katriona Maguire's role in the film which really captivated him. He was taken aback when he heard her say that she still had the very first letter she got from him. She sent him a telegram of congratulations the morning after the show. He responded, pondering on her role in his life :

"This programme should have been a tribute to the three people in my life who made my survival not only possible but worthwhile - Mother, Dr. Collis and a girl named Katriona. You present the biggest puzzle of the three, for my Mother was herself and could not help but be involved in my fate, and as a doctor and a humanitarian, it was a challenge for Dr. Collis to take a hand in my development, but I just don't know where to place you. Your duties were in the Rotunda as Almoner; they should have ended there, not in the kitchen of a poor bricklayer full of hungry kids and, sitting in the midst of them, a small thin boy with distorted limbs who looked out at you from his inner world of loneliness, and found refuge and faith. The 'courage' that so many people like to attribute to me was really nothing more than a desperate eagerness to please you. This activates me still, even if I'm not quite as romantic about it now as I was in those distant days! And at the end of it all you may derive some pleasure in knowing that you're the only woman I love quite selflessly and with utter humility. The thought of not having you there is unthinkable; it just never occurs to me. I will always need you in my life, and it seems only natural that you should always be there. It is not arrogance, or conceit, or taking anything for granted; if it is anything at all I would call it faith".

The artist at work.

CHAPTER ELEVEN

DISABLED ARTISTS : 'MY DEAR FRIEND' : THE VISITOR : CONTROVERSY.

Christy found it difficult to remember a time when he was not painting. From the age of 25 he was involved, initially as a trainee, with a world-wide organisation, the Disabled Artists Association (DAA). The DAA is a business, not directly relying on charity. Members of this organisation paint either using their feet or mouths, having lost the use of their limbs. The founding member, a German named Eric Stegmann, originally sought to have the paintings exhibited and sold through art galleries. This unfortunately did not occur. Today members earn an income through their paintings becoming popular Christmas cards, through scholarships, and grants, exhibitions and sponsorship. In Ireland Captain Sean Feehan and various family members were leading members of the DAA for many years. In the 1960s, Mary Feehan was active in establishing a roadshow of Exhibitions and Demonstrations. Christy Brown began to participate in these tours. He did not mind the public exhibitions involved though he did hate the travelling, which he found exhausting. In a 1965 letter to Katriona Maguire he said "I had to go down to bloody Ballina on Thursday on a painting exhibition, a terrible journey of nearly 400 miles in the one day".

By the mid sixties Christy had produced enough work to have notions of holding a one man exhibition, which Captain Feehan had tentatively offered to organise. He looked forward to this intensely and as time went on and nothing happened he began to write to the Captain, reminding him of his promise. In 1965 he wrote that he was very excited, saying that it would be a terrible disappointment, if his show fell though.

Early in 1965 an event occurred which caused Christy great consternation. This was the untimely death of Dr. Sheehan's husband, Bobby, who collapsed and died at the wheel of his car outside his solicitors office on St. Stephen's Green. Christy knew him very well and they had developed a great mutual rapport. On hearing of Bobby's death, Christy wrote a remarkable letter of condolence to his friend.

54 Stannaway Road,
Kimmage, Dublin 12.
April 28th 1965.

My Dear Friend,

I shall not quote cliches to you, however excellent, however well-intentioned; we are not the kind of friends who need cliches. You shall grieve the loss of your husband, your loved one, most privately and most intensely, and no one in all the world has power to lessen that grief, or has the right to, not even for love of you.

The very most we can try to do, we who care and love you in the limited human way we can love, is to keep you in the centre of our everyday consciousness, in which only then we are of any ultimate worth in the eyes of God and of man; to pray, within our limited capacity of prayer, that you may have the good grace and strength to survive and surmount this terrible Cross, the most heart-breaking you will ever be called upon to bear, with the dignity, understanding and innate goodness of soul you possess. No one in all the world can understand or share your sorrow; no facile words of comfort can alleviate your human pain. This is yours, and yours alone. Yours to live with, and die with.

We, who care for your peace and love the very wonderful person that is you, can only look on from the fringes of your life and hope for the ultimate best for you. There is much that I would wish for you; peace of mind; acceptance of whatever fate there is in life, the cheerful good humoured tolerance of life that comes only from genuine understanding: all this I would wish for you, in abundance, plus the love and admiration of those you are nearest to and hold dear. But all this is not had for the wishing; all this you will only earn by your faith and courage, by the outward flow of your active love of life in helping others not gifted with your unique heart, your singular warmth of understanding; others not gifted by being you.

Your grief is your own, all the days of your life. Let no one deprive you of it, not even out of love. Pain is inseparable from love; that is a truth we must live with. It is a proof of our true inner reality, a judgement of ourselves, as to how and with what courage we face and accept that truth. I am nothing, and because I know that, I am keenly aware of how inadequate and inarticulate my words must sound. They are not meant to comfort; only to reassure you that another shares your loss in his own inadequate way. You will not know comfort except in your own heart, in the knowledge that you have shared the best years of your life with a good man who loved you, and whom you loved with a love that will never quite be lost to either of you.

God bless and love you. Chris.

Though Christy had been associated with Disabled Artists Association for many years, it was not until 1968, shortly before his mother's death that he in fact became a full member. This had great financial implications for him. It meant that his trainee's allowance would be replaced by a payment of £140 per month. He looked forward to the opportunity to become financially independent through his art. Writing to Captain Feehan in Cork he said, "I thank you on behalf of my mother, whom I can now support with comfort in her later years. You were instrumental in giving me this opportunity and it is a debt I will never quite adequately repay you. I will work hard to prove worthy of the honour of full membership and justify my friends' faith in me".

The Association of Mouth and Foot Painting Artists, based in Vaduz, Liechestein was the group to which Christy referred. Its Articles of Association say "All members of the society...are bound to keep all negotiations, deliberations, votes etc, secret, in particular in regard to the annual results, proceeds from royalties and the assets of the Association in general. Penalties announced by the Court of Honour can be imposed for any indiscretions". The artists themselves seemed to know very little about the workings of the Company and kept quiet when asked. The monthly cheques were issued from Vaduz.

In 1968 when Christy had a batch of paintings ready for consideration by the Company, he was unclear as to where or to whom he should send them to; "to you or to Vaduz? "he wrote to Captain Feehan. He was politic enough to have already canvassed Herr Stegmann about choosing his own card. He also requested the Captain to "use your influence to have this particular picture accepted by Vaduz, as one of the Association's Christmas Cards".

Ann Jones remembers Captain Feehan's visits to their house as an agent for the Disabled Artists Association. She says the Captain used to ensure that Christy did a certain number of paintings. She recalls the family then posting the completed paintings to Liechtenstein.

It appears that there had been some public disquiet that disabled painters might be exploited in certain situations. Christy mentions this to Captain Feehan saying:

"I understand you visited the house when I was away, in connection with some undesirable publicity concocted by some university people in Dublin, allegedly crusading against the wanton exploitation of poor disabled Artists and the like...Well, I had a visit from the same gentleman shortly after I returned home, and I believe the interview went very serene indeed, I being blithely non-committal and giving them all the conventional replies to their social conscious queries. In other words, I handled them with my usual aplomb. Such zealous crusaders are irritating but synonymous with a democratic culture, which is apparently what we in Ireland are supposed to be enjoying today".

A painting entitled 'Roofs'

This controversy surfaced some years later in Britain and the Sunday Times investigated the Mouth and Foot Painters Association and its operation in England. It found that in one year alone British people contributed £3 million to the organisation. More than two million packs of cards etc were sent, unsolicited to British homes. An accompanying letter asked for up to £3.45 in return and explained that the Association was a collective of handicapped people who earn their money from these sales. Payments made in Britain went to a British subsidiary, 'Painted Postcards', which transferred receipts to Vaduz. The Sunday Times found that only sixteen Disabled British Artists benefited, of whom only eight were full-time. The Sunday Times article quoted a member of the Charities Christmas Council, Neville Bass as saying, "We have nothing to do with the Mouth and Foot Painting Association. There are faceless men behind it all. If the profits were shared out among the Artists themselves, they would be millionaires". The newspaper interviewed Peter Spencer M.B.E. , who was one of the five disabled people who met annually in Vaduz and controlled the Association. Spencer was also a friend of Brown's. Spencer told the paper "All the money goes to the Artists. We are quite satisfied with the way it is run and money is put away in an emergency fund for a rainy day. If anything happened to the company, its money would be distributed amongst the artists".

According to the Sunday Times, the Articles of the Company read quite differently[1].

CHAPTER TWELVE

LOVE FOR BETTY MOORE : WRITING IN AMERICA : IRISH LITERARY FIRMAMENT : 'A CRAZY MOSAIC' : MOTHER DIES.

In the autumn of 1965, Christy wrote to Dr. Sheehan, this time almost in a panic. Betty Moore and her husband were on a European tour. Dublin was included on their itinerary where they intended to stay for several days to see Christy! In September he wrote to Dr. Sheehan ; "I hope that you are at home and not away on holidays, because...You may remember my mentioning the friend with whom I stayed during my time in the States in 1960? Betty Moore, and I think I told you something of that story...if not, read about it in my next book!! Well, she's arriving here on Monday evening next, with her husband - (there's nothing perfect in this world!) - for five days. They are already touring Europe and Dublin will be their last stop before flying back home. I'd love you to meet her. Could you let me know...It's proving a headache just where to bring them and what to show them. They're not the usual brashy type of American tourists and don't want to do the usual pseudo-Irish things, so it will be up to me to decide for them. One thing on their list is to have a singing evening in a 'typical Dublin pub' - and I never realised until now just how untypical most of the pubs are in the city! I haven't a clue where to bring them and will just have to play it by ear - which turns out to be more fun anyway.

They are staying in a private hotel in Ballsbridge - the Mount Herbert, know it? I am quite excited naturally at the prospect of seeing Beth again after five years; we had such a lovely time of it in 1960, despite all the complications and heartbreak. We share so many interests and pleasures. I have often talked about you to her and she often inquires after you in her letters. She now teaches at some Jesuit college. Having four kids and a largeish house to look after, plus a... husband - he has ulcers - I don't know how she manages it. She's a remarkable person really. He's a perfect Southern gentleman b...!".

Mona Byrne and all the Browns, met Betty Moore during this visit. She remembers her as "a lovely person. She was a lovely lady. Her husband was also a lovely man".

Despite Christy's desperate letter to Dr. Sheehan concerning the imminent arrival of the Moores to Dublin, she was not in fact able to help him. She was unavailable at the time and never did meet Betty Moore. Instead it was Katriona Maguire who had that pleasure. Betty Moore was stunned by Katriona's beauty and surprised that Christy had not made more of it over their ten years of corresponding. Betty and her husband enjoyed the hospitality offered at the Maguire home in Dublin. This was the high point of the visit, which made Christy feel quite satisfied with his organisation of their stay.

Though Christy had often alluded to his confidants of his true feelings for Betty, he never wrote in such confessional detail about it, until shortly after their departure from Dublin. Then in a poignant letter to Katriona, he poured out his feelings:

"...Oh Katriona, life is so hideously complicated! I thought, after five years, and all that happened in between,...but nothing had changed, nothing at all. To either of us. I knew the love would still be there; that can never alter. But it is one thing to love, and quite another thing to want. And that is what surprised me, dismayed me, tormented and delighted me - that we should still want each other, not just as much, but more than ever. I had so dulled myself with both alcohol and secondary emotions over the past five years, that I thought I could meet her again and remain intact, immune; how damn wrong can you be! We both knew, from the first meeting out at the airport, that nothing had changed. It was like the first time, only more so. We were speechless. We could not bear or dare to look too long at each other, for there were others around us, including her excellent and amiable husband. It was like being swept away on an avalanche or a mighty wave; a feeling of drowning, floundering, carried away suddenly and without warning, tumultuous exultations, making you oblivious of everything else save the enchanted moment we then both shared. It wasn't all idyllic; it was sheer heartbreak, being so near, within touching distance, furtive glances, stolen touch of fingers...joyful yet utterly despairing! Once again she had changed my life completely and every other thought, every other emotion, every other attachment were submerged in the sight and sound and presence of her.

Katriona, she loves me. God knows why, but she does. She could no more lie about that than she could about being alive. She wants me, and no woman has ever wanted me like that. I suppose it is for that very selfish reason that I love her...because she loves me. I always was supremely selfish. It was a miracle so enormous that I sometimes have to pause and hold myself very still in order to realise it quite distinctly in my mind. It is a most wonderful feeling, the feeling that you are loved absolutely and without question... I was utterly heartbroken when she left; it was like going through the motions of living, like going round without a heart or mind. Nothing seemed to hold any promise any more, any meaning. For my own sake and the sake of the good people I have to live with, I plunged straight into work and I haven't really stopped since. But it was a miracle; I wasn't deluded or deceived. I find life singularly beautiful now, singularly exciting. I have rediscovered this great love, I have found it again and it is infinitely more precious to me now. I should be the happiest man alive, knowing she loves and needs me, and I would be, if only we could be together openly and forever. Whether that can ever be, neither of us know; we can only know what is, not what might have been or what might yet be, but what we share right now, and that is a love as profound as ever was between a man and a woman...We were so intensely caught up in each other that it took quite a lot of control to come down to earth and be able to cope with the conventional trappings of ordinary existence; be able to talk to people, make all the proper replies, do all the proper things without stumbling too much. I didn't quite make it as well as she, but then she has had to school herself to a routine much more rigidly than me. How we managed at all without breaking into song or openly holding hands and smiling idiotically at each other God only knows. We were both like adolescents".

He then surmises that the intense feelings between them must have been obvious to many people. He goes on:

"Now my life is geared and centred to one thing; to get back to her as quickly as possible. I'll make it, I know, within a year or eighteen months. I'll make it because I must. Nothing can stop me now. Nothing can stop us being together again, whether it is for a week, a month, a year. One thing we both know; it won't be another five years, because it cannot be. Neither of us could stand it. It would be barbaric... With me she is her true self, the woman I knew, totally involved with life, giving totally of herself, a gay, charming, humorous person, wanting only to please me and love me completely; yet a sad woman, too, knowing that we may never share the ultimate completion of our love and happiness. She looks to me for protection and reassurance. And any man who says he does not find this irresistible in a woman is a liar and a fool. For the first time in my life a woman needs me as I have always needed a woman. That alone would be a miracle, but the miracle is all the greater when the woman is such a one as Betsy, with whom alone I can be utterly happy".

Christy then goes on to say that he can only share his happiness with his friends. "I cannot share it with my Mother or my family, as much as I love them. My Mother was marvellous ; she excelled herself in making the Moores welcome and at home and endeared herself to them both. I may not give her credit for her perception and understanding, for I have the feeling she understands this situation much more than I think, and this is more to her credit, for I have told her so little. I long for the day when Betsy and I can love without secrecy or guilt; yet I dread it, too, should my Mother be still living, for it would hurt her deeply, I know, and would seem to her as if I was throwing back in her face all she had ever tried to give me and wish for me. Life and love are in constant conflict, and both are ruthless".

Before she left Dublin, Betty gave Christy a standing invitation to come and visit them again in Connecticut, especially if he continued to have difficulty with the book he was then working on. He had showed the first draft to Betty, which he realised "was awful; full of bits and pieces, no order at all and utterly confusing". Betty read it critically and saw there was potential in it, encouraging Christy to persevere. He foresaw it taking at least another two years to complete, but in writing to Katriona said, "What I need badly is editing".

Two years passed and Christy was still in grave difficulty with his writing. In desperation, though full of anticipation, in 1967, he decided to accept Betty's earlier invitation to the USA.

On this occasion it was winter and the whole environment was different. This time too it was definitely a working trip. It had been a long time since 'My Left Foot' was published, and Secker & Warburg had almost given up hope that another book would materialise. Others felt the same, believing that unless he concentrated on one medium he had little chance of producing anything worthwhile. The publishers knew that he had been working on a follow up to his original work. They had given him formal deadlines but these came and passed. Then they extended their deadline indefinitely, hoping that the wait would be worthwhile.

Beth Moore, though apparently, emotionally involved with her guest, was a strong person. She realised that Christy needed a strict regime. Because of his love for her, he submitted himself to a routine which required a certain number of words each day, before he was allowed a drink. Most of the early part of the forthcoming book was completed during this trip. Beth thought him very brave to write in such fierce detail about his family life, revealing the private horrors of that experience to public scrutiny, but advised him that he must never be afraid to write about life. She told him that what he wrote had to be clear to his audience and not just himself; that he was writing for his readers too and that they should not have to plough through verbiage, only to get a vague idea of what point he wanted to make. That was simply bad writing, she told him. This sort of direct criticism was difficult for Christy to take. But Beth persisted and insisted. She read his ongoing pages and advised about plot, characterisation, sequence of chapters and points of crisis and conflict.

Beth, Deac, Christy.

On occasions tempers became short and sulks were common. Beth controlled the drinks cabinet, and thereby controlled her guest. She bemoaned the fact that her main point of criticism, his tendency to use too many words, was going unheard. She told him that Virginia Woolfe and Dylan Thomas could write like that quite well, but he did not have the equipment or capacity for such a style. She said his writing read like a very adolescent version of James Joyce. Christy suggested that some praise would be quite welcome. Beth replied that he had got too much of that in the past, both at home and in America, with very negative results. She refused to play that role. She told him that there was something very seriously wrong with the way he was writing. She admitted that it was not incurable, but like every ailment, it could become malignant if nothing was done to prevent it spreading. Although angry at some of Beth's opinions he persevered. Eventually as the weeks passed, Beth began to be less strident as she saw some progress. At last she saw him produce what she believed to be good writing, even deserving the name of literature. She was full of excitement, saying that though she always believed he could write well, the transformation was almost unbelievable. She adverted to particular sections of the book which transformed it, proving that not alone could he write well, but that he had a talent almost approaching genius. Reading through the book today, these passages still stand out with the vibrant force of great literature. He too became aware of the transformation that was taking place in his work. He was gratified, feeling redeemed by the woman he then regarded as an extraordinary woman, and with whom he was deeply in love. He believed that he only achieved maturity during this trip. When the time came for his difficult departure, he had completed a major part of the book, to his satisfaction. This time he and Beth had created something which would remain alive for ever.

Shortly before Christmas of 1967 Christy wrote a long letter from the USA to Katriona Maguire, detailing much of his current American experience. He first declares his love affair with Dublin, despite everything America can offer

c/o The Moores
Dec. 13th. 1967

My Dear Katriona,

You must have thought I was either dead or too debauched to write. Neither, I am glad to say. I am in the best of health and spirit since coming here and having one of the best holidays anyone could wish for. These are beautiful people and I am proud and fortunate to call them my friends...

First, your letter- rather letters. It was like a breeze from over the Liffey - in one of its more odorous moods - just when I was letting myself feel lonesome and homesick, which I often do feel even in the midst of such good companionship. No, as far as I know I am not in the least Americanised, and never could be, were I to live the remainder of my days here. You didn't really expect me to be, did you? Rather the contrary for I am constantly being kidded here about my Dublin accent - at least it is Dublin to me, though it's called an Irish brogue here. I frankly never dreamed I had any kind of recognisable accent, since its bloody well hard enough as it is, to understand the purely mechanical imperfections of my speech, but now the acquisition of a brogue rather amuses me. I admire and am tremendously impressed by what I have seen so far of the American way of life, its informality and friendliness, its ready acceptance of people, its willingness to admit and abjure its own shortcomings. (Those are its virtues; its vices are something else again with which I am not entirely unacquainted, but I feel magnanimous tonight.) But, whatever about my ideals, I certainly know where my heart is. There is still only one city under the sun for me, and I love it almost because of and not merely in spite of its weaknesses, faults and glaring drawbacks. It would not altogether be impossible for me to settle down and live here in Connecticut, given the necessary financial means, working conditions and the opportunity to make a life of my own with freedom and without odium, with a girl I could love and live with and who could love and be happy with me. Given all these things I could live almost anywhere, for I am quite an adaptable creature once my mind is at peace and my heart warmed. Yet one half of me would remain in Dublin, perhaps the least attractive or productive half - I don't know, but at any rate the more enduring and uncompromising half. I would learn to live without it with less heartache, maybe, if I had someone from Dublin here with me - my good and dear friend Maura, perhaps, or my brother Sean. I do not include my Mother because it is obvious that it is not exactly the kind of relationship I had in mind, though it would be marvellous to have her here, if I were ever to settle here for any length of time, in some place of my own and the finances were steady. So my Americanisation remains unaccomplished and I remain as disgustingly and unequivocally Dublin as ever. Distance may indeed lend enchantment, but I love it as much as when I am there in it, as I do away from it; that damnable city is like some woman whom you cannot live with nor live without, and my love affair with it is one of sorrow and delighted passion".

Christy then goes on to talk about the recent death of Patrick Kavanagh and his place in Irish literature. He speaks proudly of the "new generation of Irish writers... the natural heirs to Kavanagh and Behan", Edna O'Brien, Eugene McCabe, Brian Friel, John Montague, Brendan Kennelly, John Kinsella, James Liddy, Brian Lynch, Michael Hartnett .

"Secondly, yes, the news of Paddy Kavanagh's death did indeed reach me - not through my own knowledge, for I never read the newspapers except rarely, but Beth read about it and told me. I was sorry to hear it - which you might not believe from the little bit of a poem which I wrote on hearing the sad news and which I am enclosing, but I believe in being honest and true to one's feelings even in respect of the dead, and my poem is as sincere as any that will doubtless be written in his memory. I am no judge of genius and can only praise or reject what appeals or does not appeal to my own far from perceptive or discerning taste; I do not know if Kavanagh was a genius, nor do I care. I do not know if Behan was a genius and care less. I happen to admire most of what they did, each in his own way and after his own fashion, and only incidentally acknowledge the real or transitory contribution they each made to Irish literature. Kavanagh wrote remarkably fine and moving poetry in his day, and for this he must be honoured and nobly remembered. Instead of putting up one of these stupid bloody plaques to his memory, which seems about the limit to which Ireland goes to honour her eminent men and women, I hope they do something real and of practical lasting benefit instead, like constructing a Kavanagh library or a poetry scholarship system in his name as they did eventually with Yeats. By this I do not rank Kavanagh with Yeats but neither do I rank Yeats with Kavanagh. Each stood on his own, writing out of his own spirit, each troubling that spirit into greatness that may or may not last. If, as that article you sent me said, Kavanagh knew he was immortal, then no wonder at times he was an impossible man, such an embittered man, for God knows it is hard enough to bear the thought of one's mortality without being burdened by the awareness of one's immortality, in spirit if not in flesh. I always write best myself with the comforting thought - almost the certainly - that what I am writing today will not be remembered or even read tomorrow; the possibility that it might live on would be a serious inhibition to any daring or originality I might possess. Anyway I hope his bones rest easy tonight wherever they may lie. In a way a good poet never dies and that is something to be thankful for. That is why I cannot agree with you that the Irish Literary scene is nearly dead just because most of it's leading lights are now in the clay. I know many young poets and writers who are both the natural heirs of Kavanagh and Behan and also outstanding people in their own right. There is a whole generation of new Irish poets writers and playwrights rapidly emerging and some of whom have indeed already emerged in splendid colours and with talent enough to keep the Parnassian torch flaming for many a long day to come.

There is Brian Moore from Belfast writing his brilliant sharp brooding novels of industrial Irish life; the ubiquitous, controversial, inimitable Edna O'Brien, who has yet I think to be fully recognised and appreciated as a writer of people and not merely of what people do; Eugene McCabe who is already to assume the mantle of premier dramatist of Ireland and who is almost Ibsen-like in his analysis of rural and country life; Brian Friel of course who is still young enough to be in the vanguard of this maturing generation of writers and whose comical bitter-sweet plays and stories are good enough to enthral an international audience. Among the Poets I could call many to mind without recalling their names; John Montague, Brendan Kennelly, your relation John Kinsella, my friends James Liddy and Brian Lynch, two of the best young craftsman we have today, Micheal Harnett and oh so many others whom I have met and read and found delighted discovery in. We will be hearing more and more of all those people in the next few years to keep Ireland on the literary map of the world for a while yet. Nil desperandum!

From the bones of the dead come flowers, and out of the defeated dust of Ireland come men who are alive and unafraid to record and celebrate that fact. And if there was never cause to fight for these there is always a song to sing".
Christy was obviously replying point by point to Katriona's letters, giving a report on how well Beth and Deac had looked after him over the previous three

months. He is proud of how widely he has travelled and how independent he has become.

"You want to know when I'm going home. Well, before I do that let me first tell you just what it is I've been doing here and what it has all meant to me. In the three months I've been here I have seen almost three seasons at the close of the Summer when the colours were still soft and shimmering, then came Autumn with the colours blazing and bursting out in a myriad glory of shades, taking my breath away; now it is Winter and the landscape is bare and bleak and lonely, yet with a beauty of its own, a stark beauty of line and contour that should be quite lovely when the real snow comes. While the fine warm weather lasted - and it lasted for quite a while - I went sailing with Deac and Beth and the children on their sailing boat, which has an out board motor attached. We sailed on Long Island Sound and the Connecticut River and it was thrilling. I proved quite a sailor, surprising myself again, and if ever I get rich I'm going to buy a boat and have someone sail it for me along the coast around Dublin. It's the most relaxing pleasure I know - especially when you just sit and watch other people do the work. I went to lectures and theatres and concerts and went up to Boston one weekend to see many of the historical places, including a visit to Concord, where the American Revolution began. I have been to museums and art galleries and libraries, and last weekend went up to Hartford, the capital of the State, to see the Christmas lights, which I am told are just as good as New York's, and it was indeed beautiful. On the 22nd of this month we are going to N.Y. to see "Rosencrantz and Guilderstern Are Dead, "a new play on Broadway which got rave reviews in all the papers. We will stay two days there with an artist friend of the Moores, a very brilliant man called Peter Lipman-Wolf, whom I met when he and his wife came up here for Thanksgiving. He is designing a mural for the big study downstairs. He is a splendid artist and person, and he had many kind things to say about my poems. Thanksgiving was a lovely affair with a huge turkey dinner and lots of stimulating people. I enjoyed it thoroughly. In between there have been informal parties at which I have met many interesting people and been made to feel completely at home and even a bit lionised on occasions, thank's to Beth's good reports of me and my writing.

The house itself is quite beautiful and has its own woods, about ten acres of it. It stands on a hill and has a magnificent view of the surrounding countryside. There are three stories and about 20 rooms. Beth's kitchen is a modern marvel with a gadget for almost everything. There is an elevator that takes me up and down stairs. My room is large and comfortable with a bathroom adjoining - and as you can see a lovely typewriter for my own use. Deac has put ramps down so that I have no difficulty in moving from room to room.

But it is the way in which I have come to be able to help myself that will delight you most. In fact the whole experience has been an object-lesson in physical self-education and self-help. Thanks to the ingenuity of Beth and Deac I can now do things I never did before - dressing myself almost completely, taking a bath whenever I like, feeding myself in the day-time when I am alone, brushing my teeth thoroughly each morning... you just wouldn't believe it; the dressing is made possible by means of a material called Vel-Cro, which Beth has sewn onto my shirt and pants, in parallel strips on each side which cling when pressed together. I'll show you how it is done when I get home. In fact I am just about self-contained now and can function almost independently. This I need not tell you is a tremendous boost to my morale and has put me in great spirit. I know my Mother will be delighted out of her wits at all I can do for myself now. I am dying to get home to show them all and to brag and boast unmercifully!".

Then Christy informed Katriona about how successful his writing has been. While he gives great praise to Beth's help, he is quite careful to delineate her role.

"And furthermore I have done what I really came here to do - I have finished Part One of my novel. Beth and Deac have read it, and with certain reservations and some valuable criticism, have found it very good and believe I can write quite a book. It is a great relief to have Part One behind me, and the next two parts shouldn't take nearly as long to do. Beth is going to go over the manuscript with me closely and revise it as far as possible with me before I send it on to Secker & Warburg, when I get back. Her experience as a teacher of English will be of great value, though of course she will not try to influence my prose in any way or make it more "acceptable" - an impossible task anyway, but will merely advise and suggest ways by which the book could be improved as a whole. She's been a powerful help in helping me to see things more clearly.

As for going home - this will probably be sometime in January, the first or second week. I will let you know for sure when I know myself. It will probably also be on a Sunday, round about noon, so maybe you might be able to meet me at the airport. We'll see. Things are still a bit uncertain, but I should know fairly soon and will drop you a card.

Don't worry - I am quite happy and almost blissful at times and have so far avoided the danger of either deportation or eviction. How long this will last I don't know - long enough till the time comes for me to go peacefully, I hope. Deac has been kindness itself to me, planning all kind of things to make life easier for me and make me more independent. And Beth ...has been Beth. I love this woman so much.

I haven't heard from Anne since I came here, and I don't know if this is good or bad. Give my love to Betsy and the two boys , and tell Conor I was asking after him. I hope his work continues to be interesting, keeping the national conscience virginal and unsullied by foreign trash. I have been urged again and again over here to have my poetry published, and this is something that maybe you can help me with when I get back.

My Mother went over to spend Christmas with Lil in London. I've written her with all my news. I hope she's keeping well. I worry about her. I hope this restores me in your good books. I will be home quite soon and we'll have a long, long chat together over a glass of wine. O.K.? Until then think of me and know I am often thinking of you.

All my love,
Chris".

Back in Dublin, Christy sent the completed Part One of his work to the publishers, writing "I am keeping my toes crossed that I will shortly hear good news...The paperback edition of my first book has recently been issued in the USA and I have a large correspondence from there". He doubted that the next book would command such approval. He began to develop a fixation that his new book might even be banned in Ireland. One could believe that he might have welcomed such action, as it would have put him in the company of major Irish and international literary figures.

The Irish Censorship of Publications Board was a very active body right up to the 1950s and 1960s. There was an ethos of conservatism and rigidity which continued to blight the lives and careers of promising writers. As Terence Brown of Trinity College wrote, "The only future that seemed to be open to the Irish writer in the late forties and early fifties was penury in his own country or an appeal to the wider public gallery through eccentricity, showmanship and bravado, that would distract both public and writer from the serious business of his art"[1]. Christy Brown was certainly heir to these characteristics, as he would display to a wide Irish audience in due course. It was to Beth Moore's credit, that at least on a temporary basis, she rescued her protege from such a fate. In this context Terence Brown mentions the terrible marks of indifference or misunderstanding in the careers of Patrick Kavanagh, Brian O'Nolan and Brendan Behan, all contemporaries of Christy Brown's.

After a visit to the National Gallery and the Natural History Museum in Merrion

Square, with Katriona Maguire, Christy wrote about what they had seen, making comparisons with his new work :

"Your shells, your damned, damned shells, shells from the saline edges of timeless interminable seas...Oh, you really must read Part One of this bloody besotted book. May be its the only bit of my mind that's worth reading anymore. I seem to recollect there's quite a bit in it about the mystery and mystique of sea shells, opening into a strange new fantastic world for the boy, whose naive wonderings and experiences take up the greater part of the First Part, if you see my meaning. This thing I'm doing, this book, is a kind of crazy mosaic that just about has as much relevance to literature as elephants have to the technique of ballet. I don't give a damn whether it ever sees the published light of day or not".

He notes that for the first time ever in a letter to her, he finds himself being coarse and boorish. He says he no longer can write a conventional friendly letter to her. He regards this as positive, as a sign of latent maturity.

That same summer of 1968 saw the death of Mrs Brown, the foremost of Christy Brown's women. She collapsed at home and was removed to the Meath Hospital. She was visited there by the family. Robert Collis was also in Dublin at the time and he visited her at one of his former places of work. Mrs Brown had surgery and made a brief recovery. Some days later she died and was buried alongside her husband. Dr. Sheehan says that the death came as a terrible shock to the family. They were unprepared for it, as over very many years, their mother had many serious complaints from which she always recovered. In an interview with the Word magazine, Christy remembered his mother as a marvellous woman, a great woman. Her natural intelligence and insight were marked. But it was her sense of humour he remembered her most for. She had great compassion, particularly for her husband, whom she knew, could not help the way he was. She never complained for herself. She got great spiritual comfort out of her Catholicism[2]. Robert Collis consoled Christy by advising, "don't pray for her; pray to her".

Ann Jones says of her mother: "She was an amazing woman; I mean to have such a big family and to have such a hard life and still, she had time for each and every one of us and special time for Christy, no matter what. Nowadays you wouldn't get a woman like that"[3].

The death of his mother proved a major crisis for Christy. As Mona Byrne remembers "My mother died and it left a terrible gap in Christy's life. Christy and my mother were just like that. It took so much out of him that anything could have happened, because he lay for such a long time on his couch over there in Mammy's house. He wouldn't talk, he wouldn't eat. He really went into himself. He really was bad".

Christy with his sister Ann. Courtesy Matthew Walsh.

It was clear that Christy could not live alone. Someone had to be on hand to look after him. Ann Jones, moved into Stannaway Road, becoming one of Christy's women.

Some months later Christy sent his newly composed poem entitled, 'In Memory of my Mother' to Katriona Maguire saying, "Here at last is the requiem for my mother I promised you. A poor effort, God knows. Yet in her rare indefinable way she might have said "not bad":

"Only in your dying, Lady, could I offer you a poem.
So uncommonly quiet you lay in our grieving midst
your flock of bereaved wild geese
opinioned by the pomp and paraphernalia of death
for once upon a rare time wordless
beyond the raw useless grief of your nine fine sons
the quiet weeping of your four mantillaed daughters
gathered in desperate amity around your calm requiem hour
and almost I saw you smile in happy disbelief
from the better side of the grave...

With gay uplifted finger you beckoned
and faltering I followed you down paths
I would not otherwise have known or dared
limping after you up that secret mountain
where you sang without need of voice or words.
I touched briefly the torch you held out
and bled pricked by a thorn from the black deep rose of your courage.
From the gutter of my defeated dreams

you pulled me to heights almost your own.

Only in your dying, Lady, could I offer you a poem.

I do not grieve for you
in your little square plot of indiscriminate clay
for now shall you truly dance.
O great heart
O best of all my songs
the dust be merciful upon your holy bones.

CHAPTER THIRTEEN

THE LATE LATE SHOW : 'FOR BETH' : A SHOCKING SUCCESS : A 'PRIMITIVE' PAINTER ? .

David Farrer, Christy's editor at Secker & Warburg, had dreaded reading the new book, least he might not approve and be obliged to tell Christy so. But after completing it, he said he should have believed Christy, who had promised that the book was going to be brilliant. Ann Jones described Farrer as "a meticulous man, a real English gent". Farrer would appear to have decided that Part One of the projected work, which Christy had delivered to him, was of sufficient length to merit publication in itself. The closer it came to publication date the more nervous Christy became. He tried to keep up a nonchalant front in public, but privately he feared for the fate of the book and that of himself. He was afraid his family and friends would feel he had betrayed his past. He could not bear to have anyone mention the first book, which he wanted to disown, so different was the new book going to be, though covering similar ground. He fortified himself by saying that he was only telling the truth. But he desperately wanted it to be well received. He admitted he hated criticism which badly effected his overblown ego.

September 1970 was the target date for publication. An active publicity campaign went into effect from the start of the year, to prepare the public in Ireland and Britain for this masterpiece. The Sunday Times did a lengthy piece on him. The most influential television programme on Irish television was The Late Late Show.

An appearance on that programme made one an instantly recognisable figure throughout the country. Most Irish people had heard of Christy Brown and had a very positive image of him. After his appearance on The Late Late Show all that changed. He came over as a truculent foul-mouthed braggart, to a still very much conservative population. Pan Collins was a senior researcher with the programme and later wrote a book about the Late Late Show. She writes; "A star performer on another occasion was Christy Brown; the indomitable Christy appeared on the programme and broke one of the last Irish taboos by using four-letter words on television. In fact we never have anything bleeped on the Late Late Show, and when it happened, Gay (Gay Byrne, the long-time producer and presenter) just allowed it to happen, because whatever objections there might be to other people using four-letter words, the endearing Christy could get away with almost anything. When Gay asked him 'what would you say to somebody who criticised your book harshly?', Christy replied succinctly 'f-f-f-f-fuck em'. Gay asked, 'I beg your pardon? What did you say? whereupon he repeated the phrase. I think in fact the Word was used four times during that particular programme and we didn't have any complaints at all"[1]. It is my belief that this interview, in which, Christy was as anxious as his interviewer to create a sensation, became the event which did most damage to the public perception of Christy Brown. In his own Autobiography Gay Byrne does not mention this episode in the chapter on The Late Late Show.

At this very time when Christy was on the verge of widespread fame, Katriona Maguire was still trying to place other pieces of his work around Dublin, but without success. He tried to keep up a good front with her saying that he didn't care if he did not get a half penny from the book. He just had to get it out of his system. "I don't care what they think" he said, but added that if people didn't like the book, at least they might conclude that he could write."This is what counts most of all in the end" he said.

One aspect of the publication which amused him greatly, as far as Katriona was concerned, was the possibility of the book being banned by the Irish Censor. This was by no means outside the bounds of possibility, he well realised. He used to say "I will be laughing if that happens", because the Chairman of the Censorship Board, was none other than Conor Maguire, Katriona's husband. The publication of the book in London was a fairly sober event. David Farrer recalled the trauma of first meeting Christy and the book launch, "He never talked about his ailment or his physical self in his letters, so I never appreciated before I met him how bad he was. He turned out to be not much more than an amoeba. I was horrified. For some reason as a treat for the publication of his book, we'd arranged to take him and his mother, who'd brought him over, to the Zoo and then to 'My Fair Lady'. It was a bit of a nightmare. The only person who wasn't embarrassed was Christy".

In Dublin the book was launched at a party in an upstairs room at the best known Literary pub in the city, the Baily. Des Rushe attended and wrote in the New York Times that "The room can hold 30 people comfortably and when Christy's relatives have arrived, it is crowded. Then there are friends and journalists and literary figures and hangers-on, and the place is sardine-packed. Relatives and well-wishers gathered round and showered Christy with congratulations and small talk. It is a new experience for the brothers and sisters, and it is also for Christy, who looks slightly startled at times. The brothers and sisters are well-dressed, well-behaved, decent, respectable people, and not at all like products of the novel's environment". The guest of honour in the Bailey, was the person to whom the book was dedicated, Beth Moore. The dedication read :

" FOR BETH

Who, with such gentle ferocity, finally whipped me into finishing this book...".

Beth had flown in from the USA for the occasion, which meant so much to her. She was absolutely thrilled that her endeavours had finally flowered such a fruitful result. She stayed with Katriona during her short visit. Each morning Beth rose early and drove to Stannaway Road to spend the entire day with Christy. Katriona found her a delightful and very literary person, who appeared to her to be deeply in love with Christy. The dedication on a book may often be passed over completely by the general reader, but for the author, it is an immense personal statement, which those who knew Christy, understood. It was Christy Brown's finest moment.

Christy had earlier written in a play, that "The most common name under the sun is Brown, but that doesn't mean that people with that name are either vulgar or pretentious, does it? I myself know a young chap called Brown. But he is neither a statue of vulgarity or a pillar of pretension, although he is a bit of an idiot at times. But still with all his faults and vices, I would never dream of doing away with poor old Brown. So what's in a name? Nothing, absolutely nothing. Brown - philosophy - what do they mean, if you don't know what they stand for? Put the name of Brown and - er - say Huntly-Rogerson together. At first glance one would be inclined to imagine Brown to be a Plebian soaked in poverty and ignorance, and Huntly-Rogerson to be a perfect gentleman and a shinning criterion of the aristocracy. But it may be the other way about"[2] .

'Down All the Days' very definitely confirmed that Christy was a Brown rather than a Huntley-Rogerson. As Beth Moore had earlier indicated, it told the story of brutal times and a brutalised people. It shocked the public with its portrayal of an earlier life in Dublin as vulgar, drunken and vicious. Though billed as a novel, many though it a betrayal of the private life, of his parents particularly. His good friend Dr. Sheehan felt that the book had been edited in a disjointed way, picking out the most pornographic parts, and taking away any sequence. Essentially it was a sad book, a book as Christy himself said so often, that had to be written. The language, while good to listen to, is that of sadness, a reminder of a bitter past which most people wanted to forget ever existed. He chronicled the truth of his generation in an extraordinary document, ranging from his early days in the box cart to the mid 1950' when his father died. He spared nobody, painting a vivid picture of what life was like, in a poverty stricken Dublin.

The Dublin portrayed in 'Down All the Days', like that of James Plunket's 'Strumpet City' some decades later, was of a civilisation that was almost forgotten, though still so recent. But Brown's Dublin was a great deal coarser, more outspoken, though bounded by the same preoccupations of birth, fornication and death. The physical limitations were the same, with outer surburbia and city sophistication out-of-bounds. The working class housing estate, meagre lodgings on the city quays and visits to the city cemeteries of Glasnevin and Mount Jerome, were the boundaries of this confining experience. In a violent contrast to later Dublin, nobody goes anywhere or does anything; few outside influences permeate the bread and board issues of a tight family circle. Drinking seems the main occupation with a richness of cursing, that only serves to contrast sharply the social structure in which horizon can be fixed no further than the weekend pay packet. The presence of numerous children, living, dying like rabbits or cats, are witness to the patriarchical society which makes the Father, drunk or sober, into an autocratic monster.

As Dr. Sheehan noted, the book, novel or documentary, could easily be reassembled as there was little traditional progression in the story. She writes that the book was started around Christmas 1958. She read several drafts. She also says that Christy submitted about ninety thousand words to the publishers. She felt the book, with just over thirty thousand words, did not hang together, claiming that if the parts that were omitted had been put back in, it would have been sequential. Ann Jones thought the book was "quite good. It is semi-autobiographical. It wasn't Christy writing about 'My Left Foot'; it was more about Dublin life of that particular period as he saw it". She could not recall any objections at all from the family about the book. Mona Byrne found it "a very funny book. It was more like an autobiography than 'My Left Foot'. It contained things that really happened".

For much of the book the youthful narrator speaks directly to us, though in other sections he disappears and there is no chapter sequence. For the most part, the book is a masterful scalpel-sharp descriptive work which spares no one, least of all the writer himself. There are adjectives in plenty which remind me of Beth Moore's crusade to keep them to a minimum. At one point he did threaten to go awry as he attempted a dream-like sequence a la Joyce, complete with rhyming couplets printed as prose. I can clearly visualise Beth Moore trying

The night of the Dublin launch of 'Down All The Days'
at the Maguire home in Dublin.
Front left : Katriona, Christy, Beth,

unsuccessfully to exorcise this aberration from the text. Unlike his first book, this one was amazingly free of any sentimentality, as we witness what a physical handicap entails. One sentence reads :

"He was crawling down a long dark tunnel of pain; the walls seemed about to collapse, to fold in upon him: everything seemed to be breaking up, dissolving, disintegrating: he seemed to be stuck, submerged in a sort of gum mucilage; sharp brittle points of light flashed before his eyes; into the loud confusion of his mind things swam - forceps, scissors, syringes...". This vivid language, though still tending slightly towards verbosity, is full of sharp pain which illustrates the quality of the book. The use of language is incredibly assured, marking the book out as one of the great volumes about Dublin of yesteryear.

From a literary and commercial point, the book was an immediate and huge success. It reprinted twice before publication. It sold in the region of 500,000 copies in hardback. It was translated into about fifteen languages, becoming a best-seller in most of them. It turned Christy into an international celebrity. It also made him a rich man. The reviews were excellent, generally acknowledging that it was a remarkable portrayal of Dublin slumlands of the forties and fifties.

William Trevor, reviewing the book wrote "Down All the Days, though occasionally overwritten, is an extraordinary document and one from which it might be argued that if God was cruel to Christy Brown, He also performs through him a small miracle. In the uncomplicated story there is no plot, just a knitting together of all there was down all the days of this hard life. That such a rich spate of words can come so truly and without bitterness from such a battered form is a beauty in itself, and no inconsiderable one"[3].

Those who knew Christy well were dumbstruck by his creation. They never thought it possible that he could achieve such control, such discipline, the skill to distil his bitter experience into such an unangry canvass. The absence of condemnation, no excuses from this disabled person for the losing hand he had been dealt. Even within the family and its close environs in which he wrote, there is no hint of self pity, but rather a feeling that man can survive stacked odds by concentrating on the here and now.

Of course then, and even still today, there were the doubters, those who refused to believe that the work belonged to the author. I believe, and fervently hope, that reading the letters contained in this book, one will be left in little doubt that he had the capacity for literary greatness, when he could be disciplined enough. As Katriona Maguire said of 'Down All the Days', and Beth Moore, "she disciplined him and forced him to write it".

Robert Collis wrote in praise of 'Down All the Days' and admitted that he too had only gradually discovered that Christy was an artist in his own right. For Collis the book placed Brown among the best of current Irish writers, along with Joyce and Beckett.

Collis added that 'Down All The Days' was none the less avant-garde for being accessible, unlike the masterpieces of the above mentioned gentlemen. Its terrifying clarity and truth had an extraordinary lyrical quality. The only comparison he could make of a people so vividly portrayed, was that by the great Russian novelists[4].

But the book did not win total critical acclaim. Alf MacLochlainn, while doffing the cap to the outstanding achievement of one so disabled as the author, in producing such a work, found it "episodic, lacking in thematic unity, bedevilled with cliches and superabundant adjectives and alliteration, that its local colour is off-colour". He suggested that the author could with advantage, apply Koestler's rule - cut out adjectives at the flat rate of three in five. He found the later part of the book contained some fine phantasmagoric passages far more moving than the 'realistic' first half with its "voyeuristic preoccupation with groins and body". MacLochlainn argues it is by no means clear that the cripple in the box-car has developed into the second part of the book, stating that many of the later episodes of the book could not have been witnessed by the boy.

MacLochlainn too finds fault with the topography of Dublin in the book. He says there is no river that carried turf-laiden barges through Dublin during the Emergency and no bus route which would have taken you from the Quays to Portobello Barracks via Rathgar and the South Circular Road, in that order. The critic ends with a question, "Your maiden aunt will not like the proliferation of four letter words. I had heard them all before and can only repeat a common complaint. If these words are to be the commonplaces of literary English, what are we to fall back on for our vernacular expletives? "[5].

With the wide publicity generated in anticipation of the success of the book, it had been decided opportune that a parallel exhibition of Christy's paintings might be successful. This took place in the Agnew Summerville Gallery on Duke Lane off fashionable Grafton Street in Dublin. It was difficult to get near Christy that evening as he was surrounded by television crews, photographers and social notables. The official opening was done by the noted author and wit,

Ulick O'Connor. He said that Christy's paintings breathed an inherent characteristic of Dublin life and that the portrait of his mother gave an immortal picture of Dublin womanhood. As Ulick remarked how sad it was that Mrs Brown was not present to witness her son's triumphs, a commotion occurred in the crowded gallery. It was Christy insisting vehemently that "she's here, she's here". Those present, who included Beth Moore and Katriona Maguire, were unsure whether to laugh or to weep, so they did neither. The film producer Kevin McGlory bought three of the paintings and announced that he was opening discussions with Christy on the film rights of the book. The next day Beth Moore had to return to the USA where she was to be awarded a doctorate in English literature. But their parting caused little sadness to Christy. They had earlier been to the west of Ireland and he was due to travel to Connecticut very shortly, in connection with publicity for the American edition of the book.

Brian Fallon, the chief art critic of the Irish Times reviewed the exhibition. He wrote: "...having seen his current Exhibition, I would far sooner praise his writing than his painting...As an achievement by a man severally handicapped physically, it is remarkable: judged strictly on its merits as art, it is no better than the average run of Sunday painting, except for a kind of imaginative fierceness which keeps flickering behind the limited technique and the rather wobbly drawing. Without the note of personal urgency and intensity, the pictures would be either tritely lurid or cosy.

Mr. Brown is not a 'primitive' and if he occasionally seems to be one, it is simply because he is an unprofessional artist, not because of his vision of the world. The real primitive is one who has managed to retain a child's view of things, and the vision in these pictures is an adult, as well as a rather hackneyed one.

One charming picture of boats might pass as being genuinely primitive, but I have an uneasy suspicion that this was not the intention. In fact the gap revealed in most of the work is huge - between a burning ultra-personal sensibility and a stock - not to say trite painterly vocabulary"[6].

CHAPTER FOURTEEN

VANITY FAIR : RELATIONSHIPS .

On his 1970 trip to Connecticut, where he was to spend several months, Christy travelled with his brother Sean, whom he found “grand company and marvellously adaptable”. There, he indulged himself a little with the purchase of a “motorised wheelchair, my own winged chariot” for $750, and “worth every penny. A few adjustments had to be made to bring the controls in line with my left foot, but Deac is a mechanical wizard and he did everything himself. I can work it beautifully and can now go off for ‘walks’ on my own”. He named it ‘Olympus’, “where the gods hang out because that’s how I feel right now, right here”. He wrote to Katriona Maguire:

“Life now is Elysian, Beth is near by and I am happy. There are rough bits in between, but I wouldn't miss the thorny edges for anything - they add spice to the wooing, so to speak...Guess what? Just today I went out shopping with Beth and Sean and bought myself a Norfalk jacket and shirt and rooster ties and - wait for it - yellow trousers! Yes - yellow! Crazy. I’m wearing them to N.Y. tomorrow and will slay them. Gone forever the idea of the conservative Irishman, I’m telling you...Beth sends you and Conor her love and asks to be remembered to the kids. She’s blooming. I come fully alive when she is close by. It’s extraordinary, like so many doors and windows opening, pouring in light. I’m afraid I’m a goner.

Write soon and give me all the local gossip. I so enjoyed our picnic up in the mountains that bright wind-swept day. I remember, I remember - so well. You're my special angel. Slainte!”

It is not surprising, in view of the above sentiments, and Christy’s changed economic circumstance, that he was then moving to a situation where a future with Beth was under active consideration.

Christy was being constantly sought by the American media but played hard to get for several weeks. The book was still the best seller 'back home' and was doing very well in the USA, where it had been very favourably reviewed. When eventually he did decide to grant interviews, the resulting publicity helped the sales of the book enormously. Beth entered into the publicity campaign with enthusiasm, directing and often interpreting for her protege. For the high point of the publicity campaign she and the Brown brothers drove down to New York City where Christy was to be again interviewed by David Frost. Beth was supposed to appear on the Show with Christy, but Sol Stein, Christy's American publisher, decided to substitute Sean at quite a late stage. This was a very nerve-racking experience for Sean, as he recalled in an interview with the author early in 1998. But much to his relief, he was not called on once to interpret for his brother on that Frost Show. However Sean relates that Beth was very annoyed with the substitution and complained to Christy on their return journey to Stamford. Sean did not like her attitude and it later led to a major row between he and Beth. In fact the four months Sean spent in the Moore household with his brother, were extremely difficult ones for him. He stated, "I didn't get on with Deac at all. I wasn't to their expectations. I was a bit of a hippy, I suppose".

But even for the successful author, the time eventually came, early in 1971, when he had to once more leave his beloved Beth and return to Ireland. While in America Christy had been actively considering having a new house built for himself, "preferably in or near Howth". He wanted the fruits of his labours immediately, while he was in a position to enjoy them. He was willing to bequeath his fame to posterity as long as the money rolled in, then. He was fed up of being poor. He found poverty degrading and his first aim was to escape from:

"my smelly peeling little dungeon in the concrete wilds of South West Kimmage. Poverty is no blessing. It kills love. It debases men and women. It stunts life. It withers your marrow.

Money may not be everything but by god its a hell of a lot. It may not buy happiness, as is constantly said, but whoever said it could? "[1]. If his book did bring him money, he intended to enjoy the things of the flesh more, particularly drink, declaring he would rather drown his sorrows in good porter than on Adam's ale.

Margaret Forster, the writer and wife of Hunter Davies, was among the many women with whom Christy corresponded. He had seen her photograph in a publisher's catalogue in 1965 and promptly wrote to her. They became pen pals but did not meet until 1970, and then only at his insistence. Some of his letters to her have appeared in the Sunday Times[2]. As Hunter Davies states, these letters were not written for publication - just thrown straight off, with no corrections, no typing mistakes. In them Christy plays a role of 'the broth of an Irish boy', in whose life drink is the major factor. Of his education he writes:

" What sort of education did I have ? The Beano, the Dandy, Hotspur, Captain Marvel: all of these erudite publications were high on my reading list as a child and later as an overgrown boy. At an advanced age (17) - I encountered

Dickens one fine day and he has ruined my prose ever since. Yes - I did, briefly, have a tutor once, paid for by certain other illuminous but misguided souls, who tried valiantly to civilise me and inculcate in me a love of learning. But the effort proved too much for the good man and he died from a brain haemorrage"[3].

Christy used some of his new found wealth to purchase 54 Stannaway Road and give it to one of his brothers. His idea of moving to Howth did not materialise, as it would have been extremely costly and the wrong side of the city for his family. Instead he had two interconnecting bungalows built in the village of Rathcoole, about fifteen miles in the west of County Dublin on the Wicklow border. He asked Ann Jones, who lived with her family in the Browns of Stannaway Road to transfer to Rathcoole and look after him there. Ann moved with her family into one of the houses and Christy occupied the other. He found the transition to the countryside marvellous. He felt he had more freedom and independence there. He was removed from his background but thought that was probably a good thing, hoping it would be conducive to good writing. He believed it would enable him to be more objective. Rathcoole gave him peace and plenty of time to think, though he admitted that one part of him would always be in the city.

The two bungalows at Rathcoole.

The new house was bright and spacious. It had certain adaptations made to enable Christy to function more easily and independently. The doors were sliding, with handles at ground level, as were all the electric switches and plugs. It had a sunken bath, which he could access to and from. Automatic dryers overcame the necessity for towels and a bidet assisted with his toilet regime.

Although close to Ann and her family, who were very good to him, Christy sometimes felt very alone, particularly at night. After Ann and her husband would retire for the night, he would make his way back to his own house where he would try to write. When that proved difficult he would often pass the night drinking, listening to music and contemplating his isolation.

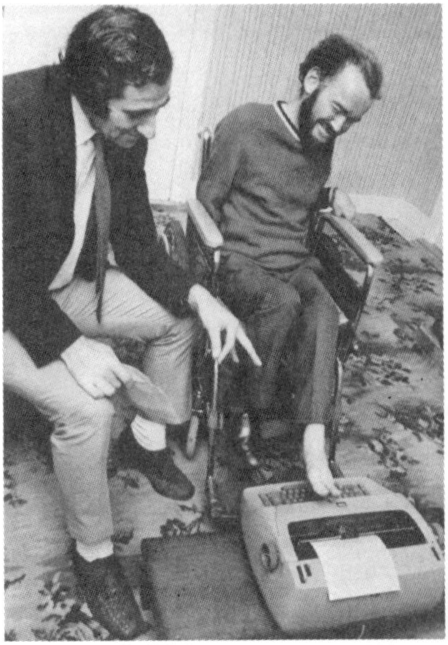

Des Rushe with Christy
(Courtesy Matthew Walsh)

The journalist Des Rushe visited Christy in Rathcoole and wrote in the New York Times of 28 October 1971 of the physical technique involved in Christy's writing: "At work he sits before an electric typewriter that rests on an oblong bench scarcely 12 inches off the floor, a length of wire trailing from the machine to a socket in the wall near the fireplace. His left foot ranges over the keyboard, the little toe picking out the letters, the big toe tapping the space bar. The in-between toes are idle. The fingers of his right arm are twined round an armrest support in such a way as to give him some leverage. His stunted left hand rests tentatively somewhere near the back of the wheelchair. His slight body is perennially contorted. The little toe picks out the words laboriously, vainly trying to keep pace with the composing mind, now awhirl with the words of a novel-in-progress. His body writhes in irritation and he tosses his head with coltlike impatience - a Pegasus eager to keep abreast of the flight of thought but absurdly tethered to an inadequate little toe. Eventually he reaches the end of typed sheet, and with a deft movement of the big and second toes, he removes it and places it on a small pile of recently-completed manuscript. As he manipulates another sheet of typing paper into place, he runs his toes over the typewriter in a gentle caress. It is a wistful gesture". Ann Jones was present in the room with Rushe. Christy spoke of the close and strong bond between them but Rushe reports Christy saying that "if a choice had to be made between Ann and his typewriter, he would choose his typewriter. He has a look of desperate seriousness when he says it, and Ann is slightly startled". Rushe adds some quotes from the manuscript which identify it as Christy's next published novel, set in America, in which he declares that he would never sacrifice his typewriter for any woman.

Christy had been writing poetry, or his brand of poetry, as he put it in 1956, for many years. On one of his trips to the USA some of his poetry was read publicly. There was a plan to publish about fifty of them there. These were also to be translated into German. He wanted to be a poet more than anything else. He once wrote to Mrs Maguire saying;

" Oh Caitriona, do you think I will ever be a poet? To me life is extraordinarily beautiful, and I want to sing about it, but at times I feel like a bird, trapped in a cage, without wings or voice".

He felt that poetry was his best way of communicating and he gained more pleasure from poetry than any other medium. Now that he had firmly established his name, this was the medium in which he was next published.

A collection of his poems was published just a year after the book. It was called "Come Softly to My Wake" and dedicated to Ann Jones. He told her that the dedication was "for helping to keep the ship afloat", since she had been the one looking after him lately. Though he was eleven years older than her, they had a great relationship. The age difference mattered only when they were young. As Ann says, "age is only a number".

The first edition of "Come Softly To My Wake" consisted of five thousand copies. It sold out within weeks. It contained thirty seven poems. This collection was memorable for its last five poems. One entitled 'Brendan', commemorated his erstwhile drinking colleague Brendan Behan. It is a romantic attempt to revivify the larger than life, though very sad and wasteful career of Behan, portraying him as the master clown in so many Dublin locations:

> " his gorgon's head and cherub's face
> swimming into view over the pint tops".

'A Kind of Lament' is a more restrained effort to remember Patrick Kavanagh, as he too conducted his own odyssey through Dublin city:

" striding with shoes untied through singing streets
of a lost city that never called you son."

'For My Mother', which he had sent to Mrs Maguire shortly after completing it a few years earlier, is a totally self-indulgent poem, demonstrating Brown at his least controlled craftsmanship. Yet read as his thanks to her, celebrating her life, it has an enduring strength. He declared that, only when she was dead could he offer his mother a poem.

Eileen O'Cuilleanain found this collection of poems 'loose and emotional. They contain evidence of strong feeling, humour and exact observation, but the language and ideas have not been thoroughly sorted out by a poetic discipline. Thus, a number of elegies become merely a succession of descriptive phrases, fine in themselves but not adding up to a whole poem. Brief sketches like "Sunday Morning" and " Spring" are more successful, with acutely noticed satiric or physical details, as with :

"They troop by in twos and threes
with covered heads and covered knees
scented bright queenly exteriors
matted eyelashes and articulate posteriors.
Sunday Morning.'[4].

This book too continued his writing explicitly about sexual matters, particularly masturbation. Many people have difficulty in coping with their sexual nature. For disabled people this is especially so. Their sexual maturation is normal as is their desire for sexual fulfilment. But the possibility of their achieving that is very limited. Hence for them, matters sexual may loom larger than for the abled. Often a complex may develop and sex or the lack of it, can be at the forefront of their thoughts.

It can become a constant topic of conversation. Life can become a battle to achieve sexual experience. Self gratification may become the only possible way. This road though, only leads to more frustration and negative self indulgence. As Brown wrote in 'Routine', in the same volume, a pattern can develop which takes over and though one may regret it, after the act, tomorrow will bring a repeat performance:

"There's no use crying over spilt sperm.
What I do and regret today
I'll do and regret tomorrow
and whatever other tomorrow I may see
with undiminished intensity"

The disabled can even become more boastful about their real or imagined sexual experiences than the abled. Their frustration, once released, may give rise to a lack of inhibition. Often a sense of bravado and even an attempt to get their own back on the abled can lead to attempts at being shocking or exhibitionistic. This was very evident in Brown's writings and is almost puerile to the outside observer. Yet because society treats disabled people differently, in an almost antiseptic way, this was tolerated in him, if not encouraged.

People with physical disabilities, form a distinguishable minority which is discriminated against in a multitude of ways. This is true today, but was much more so in Christy Brown's time. He was not afforded the service of a clear medical diagnosis and appropriate therapeutic intervention as an infant, when he might have benefited. He was rejected by the educational service which did not feel capable of meeting his needs. Even his Church felt that he could not be treated like the rest of its congregation.

These insults, though painful, were more easily acceptable than those which were personalized, because of their institutionalised nature. Disabled people find themselves rejected in thousands of little ways during their lives; little ways, because people are generally kind and try to avoid hurting by keeping the disabled at a distance, a distance safe for themselves. As a result disabled people are further discriminated against in their desire to mature personally. They quickly learn to adapt to what is expected of them; they recognise the demarcation lines which society and individuals place around themselves. The disabled make contact, but only at a certain level, rarely as full person to person. Disabled people may be poor economically and spiritually and learn to accept charity from the do-gooders of the voluntary and professional varieties. Their needs, desires, ambitions are the same as the rest of society however. They want to be successful, they want to love and be loved. They spend their lives searching, watching, hoping for such an opportunity. They are hurt, abused and rejected. But they remain human and if they do succeed, they wish to put the horrors of the past behind them, as quickly as possible. They want to scatter their traces. Unfortunately, such successes are very rare so far, but Christy Brown was in that vanguard.

Disability, especially in the conservative ethos of institutional care, almost always meant a total deprivation of inter gender sex. Catholic morality also contributed, in that what might be physically possible in the sexual sphere for some disabled, might be outside the accepted moral code. Christy Brown was not to be so entrapped. He portrayed himself as an experienced youth and man in sexual matters. He said that casual sex left him dreadfully unfulfilled and empty. He found that the saddest part about the so-called permissive age, was that things like sex lose their beauty. He believed that pornography had taken all the mystery and beauty out of the human body[5].

Women are often very attracted to disabled males. Their vulnerability, their helplessness, brings out a special maternal and caring instinct in women. Disabled youths and men crave after female company and companionship. They offer an emotional bond to women who do not see them as sexual beings. Close relationships can develop in which the partners feel at completely different levels of commitment. Then if sex does become a factor, it can shatter the illusions created, leaving both parties wounded. The abled though, usually have a better chance of recovery in a more normal and natural relationship, as they might view it, in a defence mechanism. Marriage and an independent home and economic life, are the ultimate aims of most abled and disabled people.

Christy Brown was no exception, having experienced the gamut of all the possible kinds of relationships with the abled since his childhood, and when that opportunity came he had no hesitation in taking it.

Dr. Patricia Sheehan has spoken of the difficulty of disabled clients establishing relationships with those providing services, in the context of Christy Brown. She says : "Christy brought out all the maternal instincts in caring for someone who needed looking after, although he was an independent bod in his own way. Women had a large part in his life. You meet someone in a setting and you're either a therapist or a carer. It's very difficult to change the direction of a relationship once it's been established and then try to become affectionate or romantic. The familiarity of meeting then brings out the natural lustful inclination of the client. It's very difficult to have had someone who's pushed you a half hour a day and then you suddenly want to kiss them or grab them. It's very difficult to change the momentum of a relationship. It's like a bereavement"[6].

CHAPTER 15

MARY BROWN : THE COLLIS STORY : A NOTABLE WEDDING: 'THE MAJOR MIRACLE' OF HIS LIFE'.

In 1969 Christy had been invited to appear on the 'David Frost' television Show in London. The interview proved a great success and the experience was thoroughly enjoyed by Christy, who described his host as, "great and witty". Afterwards one of his brothers, Sean, who lived in Bayswater gave a party to celebrate Christy's visit. Christy was, as he said himself, "unbelievably undrunk", when he noticed a lady sitting on the opposite side of the room. She did not appear to be joining in the general conversation around her. Christy began to glance her way from time to time, until she became the one interesting person in the overcrowded room. As he saw her begin to socialise, a great loneliness overcame him, and try as he might he was not able to get drunk. The lady in question, was a friend of a friend of Sean Brown's, who had invited her to the party. She of course had noticed the guest of honour and was aware of how alone and bored he seemed to be. Her friend encouraged her to go over and speak to him. She sat down beside him on the sofa and asked him how was he enjoying the party. She said she believed he was a writer. Christy had worked himself up into such a state that he wasn't able to conduct a normal conversation. He was so excited that the lady with the entrancing blue eyes and an eminently kissable mouth, set in a face worthy of Botticelli, was talking to him, that he tried to impress her by demonstrating how widely read he was in the Anglo-Irish poets. She was able to understand his speech perfectly. Her name was Mary Carr. She was a native of county Kerry and had lived in Tralee to the age of seven. She remembers Christy as a rather good-looking man with curly brown hair, a neatly trimmed moustache and beard framed sensitive face. His deep blue eyes radiated an electric compassionate intelligence[1]. He was thirty six and she twenty three years old.

After their initial and rather strained meeting, Mary found Christy to be a very vivacious person, quite amusing with a great sense of humour. Christy wrote to every beautiful female he met and Mary Carr was no exception. She replied to his letter and very soon a regular correspondence developed. When he returned to London for the launch of "Down all the Days" in 1970, they met again. His honesty and gentleness impressed her.

Back in Connecticut, Beth was having a difficult time, as it became clearer what Christy's long-term intentions might be. She wrote to Christy giving him a graphic description of her domestic situation. The realisation of what might be planned did not find favour with Deac, who had been so good to Christy over so many years. He declared that he never wanted to meet him again. He feared for himself and his children, least their privacy be invaded in a forthcoming book by Christy. Both Deac and Beth knew that Christy had a new book in hand, which dealt with his American experience. Christy himself described it in an interview with the journalist Des Rushe, "Yes. It's completely different to Down All The Days, much more objective. The location is the United States, where I've been four or five times. The book combines all the visits in one experience".

Christy wrote to Beth insisting that she must trust him in their situation. But this advice was of little comfort to her. She wrote in a very sad letter of May 1971, to Christy, that she was exhausted and discouraged.

Christy and Beth had planned to spend some time together later that summer. She was surprised to get a letter from him, stating that it would be essential for them to spend at least a month together in Ireland. This caused surprise to Beth. She felt that Christy must have been taking advice from a third party. She recounted all the time they had spent together over the years and told him that he had ample opportunity to know everything about her. She said that when they met in August they would have to do some serious talking.

Beth came to London in August and stayed at the Rubens Hotel in Victoria. She hired a car and spent a few weeks touring the countryside with Christy. It became clear subsequently that Beth's earlier suspicions were accurate. Christy was indeed considering his options and Mary Carr was very much in his thoughts at that very time. He had known Mary for about two years and found her extremely attractive. She was also very interested in him. There is no record of Beth and Christy ever meeting again after their English holiday of August 1971, though at least one further letter passed between them.

When I asked Sean Brown if he had any sympathy for Beth in that situation. Despite their differences he replied, "a little, I suppose. But I admired the woman for what she did for Christy. He had never left the country before. He had never left his family before. She was willing for him to go and stay with her family in America; feed him, wash him, look after him, which his family had to do. That was one of the good things about her. In regards to his writing, she did give him a lot of help. He used to write to her, asking what do you think of that, do you agree with this. She would write back in long letters. She helped him. She gave him a lot of confidence".

The opinion of the author is that Beth Moore acted honourably with Christy at all times. She played an essential role in the writing of 'Down All The Days'. She displayed an openness, even a naivety, which is common to many successful Americans. This is not a familiar characteristic in Irish people and she was therefore vulnerable. When the opportunity came and Christy was in a position to put another chapter of his past behind him, he had no difficulty in doing so. Beth Moore, to her eternal credit, was one of the most important of Christy Brown's women.

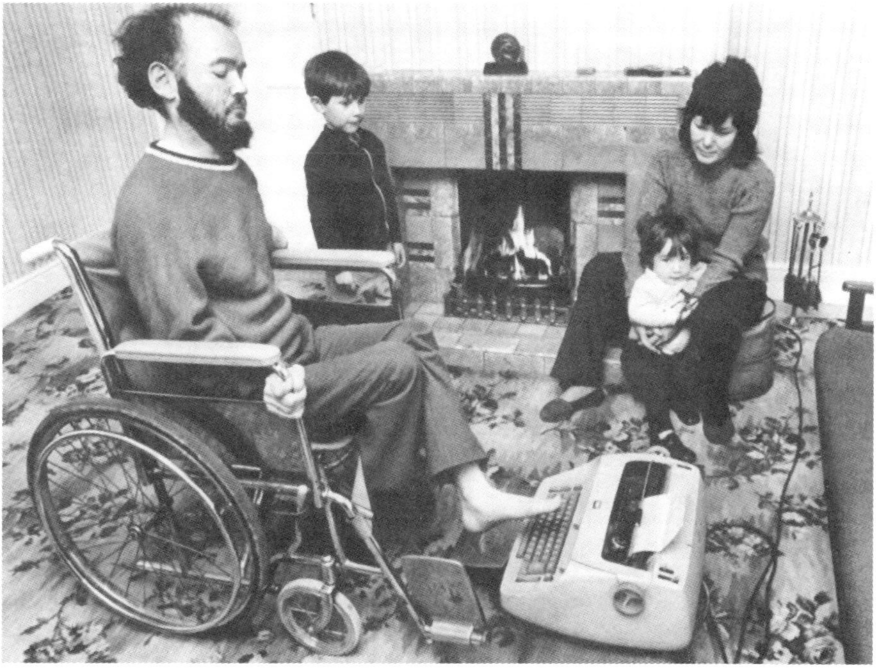

Christy with Ann and her children
(Courtesy Matthew Walsh)

Not long afterwards, Christy, in the interview with Des Rushe referred to above, spoke publicly of Mary without identifying her. He said that he had this rather beautiful relationship with a person. He loved her and she loved him. He wanted to be with her all the time. He regarded it as the best thing that ever happened to him, but admitted that all deep relationships had their despairing moments. When asked would he marry her, he replied that it was not possible. He longed to marry but then doubted whether he would. He realised that such a marriage would not be easy for a woman because he regarded himself as a very difficult person to live with. A marriage partner for him would face enormous psychological and emotional demands[2]. He did not however envisage his disability as presenting an insurmountable handicap to marriage.

When Christy made his inevitable proposal of marriage to Mary, she was shocked and wondered if he was serious. She came to visit him at Rathcoole several times. Then shortly before Easter of 1972 she again visited and this time brought a friend with her. It was then that Mary and Christy became engaged and planned to marry in October. The news did not surprise Katriona Maguire as she had always known that it was what he wanted most. But when she visited Rathcoole that same Easter and Christy informed her that he was engaged to Mary, Katriona didn't believe him at first and sought confirmation from his sister Ann.

Of course Christy's new love affair was of major import for Beth Moore in Connecticut. They had been in constant communication for more than fifteen years. He had acknowledged her major role in writing 'Down All The Days'. The long trans-Atlantic relationship between them had not been easy for either party. He persevered in it because on each occasion they were together, he found the strength of their mutual love shone forth and fortified him. It continued to be for him, a major stabilising factor in his difficult life. But all along the one thing he craved most of all was the opportunity to marry. When this opportunity came so readily and without major complications, he had little difficulty in choosing Mary. He had earlier written of Beth, "I suppose it is for that very selfish reason that I love her...because she loves me...I was always supremely selfish".

Sean Brown, who regarded Beth and Deac highly, for all they had done for his brother, is of the opinion that despite Christy's protestations, Beth was not in love with him. He saw no future in their relationship and was not surprised that Christy's main ambition remained to be married. I prefer Katriona Maguire's opinion and the evidence of the letters, that Beth did indeed love Christy. The harshness of his life had made him tough and given him the ability to make decisions about people, which were in his own self-interest. With their relationship terminated, Beth's thoughts turned to self-protection and she sought the return or destruction of her letters. When this did not happen, she began to fear for her own and her family's privacy, knowing well that the novel he was currently writing was based on his experiences in America.

Some of Christy's own family and some of Mary's friends were not overjoyed by the news of the impending marriage. Christy consulted his brother Sean, who advised him against the marriage. Sean said that Christy was so much in love with Mary that he ignored his advice. Up to then Mary felt accepted and welcomed by the family. "I wanted so much to be accepted, to be loved by them, to be a part, probably because my own family had gone away. But instead of an in-law, I was seen as an out-law. It seemed that as soon as they realised Christy was serious about me, they stopped liking me", Mary has said[3].

Mona Byrne's recollection is that "Mary was as welcome into the family as the rest of the in-laws". She felt it was a good thing that Christy got married, especially after their mother had died.

Ann Jones had never visualised Christy getting married, but admitted that Christy was the type of person who fell in love with every girl he met. When it happened, she was delighted for him because he always wanted to be like the rest of the lads. Some objections to the impending marriage were based on the fact that Mary was a divorcee. The couple received a stream of anonymous letters and phone calls. They were told that "Christy's mother would be turning in her grave"[4], since their marriage would take place in a Registry Office and not in a Catholic church.

Christy believed that his mother, though a devout Catholic herself, sensed and accepted that the trappings of institutionalised religion became pointless for him. For her sake he had tolerated the monthly visits to the house of a priest, to hear his confession, but terminated these as soon as his Mother died. He was not proud or cynical about being non-religious.

He just accepted that some people, particularly women, had a greater capacity for spiritual belief. He respected religion and was not an atheist. He believed in God, accepting that there must be a Supreme Being. Otherwise,he thought he would go mad[5]. He tried to keep emotion out of his life and as religion made him very emotional, he kept away from it. He believed that God did not object to that.

* * * * * * * * * *

Dr. Robert Collis too, had a consultation with Christy about his marriage. But it is again necessary to give an update on the life of Robert Collis, who had returned from Africa a year earlier in tragic circumstances. His career had gone extremely successfully in Nigeria. After spending five years in Ibadan he became Professor at the University of Lagos in 1962 and Director of the

Institute of Child Health of Nigeria. Later he became Professor and Clinical Dean of Bello University in Kaduna and Zaria in Northern Nigeria. In a 1962 letter to Katriona Maguire, Christy wrote: "...I had a letter just this morning from Bob Collis, still immersed in his Nigerian adventure...He says his wife Han and their two sons are doing well and thriving, but as always he professes a deep longing to be back in Ireland with all his old friends, something now sadly quite remote and improbable, I should think...I miss Collis greatly ; he was such an anchor to me, at once a father and a big brother, even if at times he succeeded in making me feel like a very amateur pupil at the feet of Socrates - which no doubt I was".

Robert Collis, Founder of Cerebral Palsy Ireland (1900-1975)

Collis invited Dr. Sheehan out to Lagos at Christmas of 1966 to advise on how to stimulate his son Niall to talk. She later told John Quinn of RTE in an interview on her education that "There was very little I could do. The little fellow was very handicapped - he had a multiplicity of problems".

Sean Collis the eldest boy of the second marriage, spent his Christmas holidays of 1968 in Zaria with his parents. Then he went back to Ireland to his boarding school in Waterford. On 9 April 1969 Collis got a message saying that Sean had been killed in an accident. Both parents were devastated. They arrived back in Ireland to be met by Zoltan Collis, one of the children they had brought from Belsen and adopted. Zoltan had completed all the funeral arrangements.

Christy Brown commemorated the boy's death with a poem dedicated 'For Han and Bob':

> "You who went so innocently before us
> do not forget us in that green-gold world of yours.
> You the gay laugh upon the Wicklow wind
> smiling boy upon a rainbow."

Within eighteen months, Robert and Han had left the turmoil of Nigeria and returned to Ireland. Soon Collis was very pleased to find that his services were being requested again. He was asked to act as examiner in the medical finals in both of the universities in Dublin. He rejoined the Board of The National Association of Cerebral Palsy which appointed him as consultant, with the task of reorganising their services and writing a national plan for services for the physically handicapped in Ireland.

* * * * *

As we have seen despite his long sojourn in Nigeria, Collis had kept in touch with Christy through his annual visits to Dublin. Now he felt obliged to speak with him, about the pending marriage. He was very sceptical about the prospects. He foresaw a difficult marriage, particularly with the problems Mary would encounter, coping with Christy's physical disability. He also felt that marrying a genius would not be easy. Collis, in his usual brusque manner, spoke to Christy about how he felt[6]. Christy reassured him that Mary would be a match for the task of making him a happy man. He assured Collis that the couple had talked extensively about their future together. He did not think that Mary had any misgivings about the step. He regarded her honesty and intelligence too highly, to think that she would marry him if she had any doubts. He believed that it was genuine love on both their parts.

They were married as planned in October 1972. At the Registry Office in Molesworth Street, Christy signed the register with his left foot. He joked that marriage in a registry office would make it easier to terminate the marriage, should that ever prove necessary. The wedding reception was held at Sutton House in Howth. It was a great public occasion attended by all his family and friends. Katriona Maguire was a guest at the Brown family table. Several notables including Charles Haughey, Gay Byrne, Richard Harris and Niall Tobin attended. David Farrer, his editor from Secker, also was there. Christy described the event as the most unnerving of his life. Weddings can be occasions fraught with tension. When a member of a large closely knit family marries, it is a major event for the family and sometimes a traumatic one. Marriage brings changes to all previous relationships. There can be hurt and recrimination before time and distance smooth ruffled sensibilities. For the Browns it was not such a shattering experience as after a honeymoon in the Bahamas, Christy and Mary returned to live side by side again, with his sister Ann Jones in Rathcoole. He was glad to get back from the monotony of the perfect weather of the Carribean, which soon had him pining for a drop of Irish rain. This time, he had with him, "the major miracle" of his life, the last of Christy Brown's women.

CHAPTER 16.

SUBURBAN DUBLIN : RURAL KERRY : CUTTING LINKS : COLLIS AND THE CEREBRAL PALSY ASSOCIATION : ' SHIT UP MR. BROWN ' .

The major adjustment in life fell to the new Mrs Mary Brown. The enormity of the move she made cannot be overestimated. Her love for her husband knew no bounds, as it made her abandon her life in London and undertake to live in future with and for her husband.

He could not lavish enough love and praise on her. "After decades of mediocre and practically sexless bachelorhood", he was married to "a stunningly beautiful woman". Though he did find the new experience of sharing a bed all night long, very difficult. It was so unfamiliar that it made him ill at ease initially. He said his wife was also "a homemaker who could sew, make beds, hoover, wash, iron, cook exceptionally well, drive their car". What he enjoyed most of all, "was in the evenings, he had someone to talk to, to share a bottle of wine with, someone who would not be leaving him". She sought to organise and stabilise their home setting, so that he could get on with his writing.

Mary soon found Rathcoole too suburban. Though it was out in the country, housing estates had been built nearby. During the day housewives and their children abounded. "There was just nothing but women and prams. You couldn't bring Christy for a walk anywhere without bumping into a pram" she said. Mary also found that they had a never-ending stream of visitors. She began to feel that Christy was almost regarded as public property, to be viewed, interviewed and photographed. His legion drinking companions had come to regard Rathcoole as an open house, where drink could always be guaranteed." They thought Christy was on a permanent holiday" Mary said[1]. Paradoxically Christy often felt that some people who had been very close friends and allies had changed their attitude to him. He felt that they thought he had outgrown them and become even big-headed, due to his success. Some were envious and suspicious. He was saddened by all this, but could not afford to let it worry him.

Mary gradually began to feel that if Christy was to get any serious opportunity to finish the novel he was working on, they would have to get more privacy. She began to think of the country, particularly where her own roots lay, down in county Kerry. Ann Jones recalls that they spent quite some time going up and down the country, searching for a place. She feels the fact that Mary was from Kerry made the choice for them.

Before they moved out of Dublin, Christy was putting the final touches to a new collection of poetry which was published in 1973. This was called "Background Music" and was dedicated, "For Mab, Herself My Best poem, and My Wife". It was memorable for two poems, one of which commemorated his brothers. The other poem named "Good Friday", distiled the Christian religious experience for all believers. It also clearly showed the depth of the writer's own faith:

> "Sunk in the agony of betrayal, His denied majesty
> A crown of thorns girding the tranquil brow ;
> And there, Fatherless, they nailed Him to a beam of mountain wood,
> And the pain-bright eyes gazed into the deeps of all that had been and was yet to be..."

After about two years of married life in Rathcoole, the Browns bought and renovated a cliff top cottage about a mile outside Ballyheigue village, ten miles north of Tralee in county Kerry.

Christy christened it "Mab Cottage". It was nearly as far as they could move from his Dublin background and remain within the country. At last the couple could be truly on their own. Their intention was to live a quiet life and let Christy get on with his work. To move from an urban environment to a rural one takes adjustment for anybody. But the man from Kimmage was nothing if not adaptable and he loved the country, especially the quietness.

They did not intend at the time to have a family. They were completely enamoured of each other, feeling that they were a self-contained family unit. As Mary said, "I don't think it was on the cards really. I think we were too caught up in each other to have anybody else around"[2]. She said Christy enjoyed the domesticity. He was interested in shopping and cooking. He asked for very little and never demanded much out of their relationship. He used tell her that he loved her as many as twenty times a day. Their relationship was more emotional than sexual. He treated her as if he was another woman. He was not possessive of her. He gave her plenty of freedom. He was never worried she would have an affair[3]. But the happy couple were quite human, Mary has said. They had their rows. He was given to outbursts of anger and frustration. He was always angry about his disability. Sometimes their differences would include, "a real old Kerry ding with fisticuffs; but usually they both would end it, in a good uniting flood of tears"[4].

They usually went out to dinner once a month. Mary would naturally have to feed her husband. As she said, "People would be agape and several times asked to be moved. They can't cope with the fact, I think, that there's something out of the ordinary. It's just like women breast-feeding. People are embarrassed. They look the other way". Life with Christy meant handling his bursts of frustration and anger. Mary said, "He used to get terribly bored.

This is what you had to watch. If he got bored he'd go on the sauce, or he'd get frustrated and write something stupid, for the crack. He would get frustrated with other people, but would also get very angry with himself...he was always angry about his disability...He'd show you up in public if he didn't get his own way. He used to stamp his foot and say, 'give it to me', so you more or less had to"[5]. He was after all a rich and famous author, much sought out for interviews with reputable media sources. To have achieved so much and yet to be so helpless, was an apparent contradiction, which did not lessen with time. He longed to be his own man.

In literary terms, Christy still realised the huge debt he owed to Beth Moore for her work with him, on 'Down all the Days'. This weighed on his mind, as just one more example of how he always found himself beholden to somebody else for whatever he achieved. That the public felt like that too, annoyed him. He wanted to be recognised for his own worth.

He decided in his next novel to reject his literary mentor and create his own fashion. He would be no acolyte of any brave forgiving woman. At the end of everything, he wrote, they could only look at each other, like two unhappy strangers, who had shared a certain short unscheduled journey together, without anything but the most ordinary words passing between them. The story line of the new book, must have hurt Beth Moore and her family deeply, but it was indicative of how selfish, even ruthless, Christy could be, when he felt such action was demanded. This exorcism is what he attempted in "A Shadow on Summer", published in 1974. It carried the dedication ; "For Mab, deliverer of all my dreams, taking me ever towards morning". Christy felt that he could not hope for the same financial success as with his previous novel. He declared himself happy to settle for critical accolades, if need be.

The book was set in New England and appeared to be based on his experiences there. It was later read with incredulity, by one very close to Christy, who also had reason to have a very high opinion of Beth. That person was staggered that he could have been so hurtful to the woman whom she believed, had loved and done so much for him. She felt the greatest wrong was to appear to have invaded a family's privacy.

Far from creating a worthwhile independent literary text, the book was a sad reversal into his old bad habits. It cried out for what Beth Moore called for in earlier times - a restraint with words. He makes the New England hostess say to the visiting disabled author, "the talent you have is like, Riley - it needs constant care, constant pruning, it cannot be allowed to be choked in a proliferating wilderness of language"[6]. Unfortunately the new novel was exactly that, prodigally overwritten. As he has another character say, "It's good and it's lousy, sometimes almost great and quite often appalling". The opening sentence of the book which contains sixty six words illustrates his cliches and usage of too many adjectives. One could almost believe this novel is an attempted caricature of how Christy Brown was supposed not to write. The editorial control of David Farrer, who allowed the book into print must also be questioned. But then at that stage Christy Brown was a household name, a commodity in the literary-commercial world, who was guaranteed a certain success for whatever he produced.

The novel concerned the adventures of an interesting cripple called Riley McCombe, born and bred in the Dublin slums, who writes a smashing best-seller and arrives in New York to be pushed, exploited and publicised and coddled and cuddled into writing another best-seller. He is detailed to stay with the Emersons, who have a nice little place near the sea somewhere between Grand Central and the suburbia of southern Connecticut.

Laurie Emerson, the wife, is beautiful and intelligent, though her literary comments do sound rather like the out-pouring of an earnest first-year college student. She falls in love with Riley, who has a thin hawk-like face and seems to have, in spite of his crutches, what the girls need. Laurie becomes his muse, his mentor and a tentative passion springs up between them. She constantly offers a running commentary of advice and encouragement which comes over, not by accident, as overpowering. But Riley is caught in an impasse, which appears to this author, a clear exercise in rationalisation and self-justification, when he writes that he is torn between what he feels for Laurie and the fact that the world sees him only as her creation. For many, "Laurie was moulding and re-making him into the creature he was to become, fashioning him with that alert keenly honed quicksilver intellect of hers into a sensitive industrious being, with a sizable mantle of success about him, a primitive come down from the mountain to this suburban haven of exquisite manners and fastidious learning, to be neatly trimmed and groomed and slotted into his predestined cubbyhole to which Laurie alone held the key... So his love for her battled with this resentment of the role, real or imagined, that she played in his life".

Laurie's husband, a patient domesticated man, then begins to grow jealous of Riley. His daughter tells Riley that her Daddy fears he is losing his wife and she is losing her mother. Eventually the husband confronts Riley, in the presence of his own wife, to her utmost embarrassment. Among the matters the husband says to Riley are, "I bet you'd even have the arrogance to die young - you couldn't resist such a great publicity stunt like that...you are first and foremost the egotist par excellence, the opportunist supreme, your own best publicity agent...".

In a mood of self-revelation Riley rebels against this glittering world and his femme fatale, deciding to return to where he came from. He says, "If he had to have dreams, if he had to speak his dreams, it would not be to any printing machine, it would not be to any brave forgiving woman, no he would sell his dreams to the mad wind scudding over his scarecrow mind, to the working-man's friends, the dogs and the sparrows, the horse tethered to the stupid hands of men, the swans who graced the filthy canals with their sad proud loveliness".

Mary Manning wrote of "this modish book" thus: "That he has talent is certain, that he has taste is doubtful, and that he maintains his artistic integrity is now in the balance. I will not do him the indignity of judging his work any more as the outpouring of a freakish wonder. He has set himself squarely in the arena of the writing world and he must be judged on those terms. Sean O'Casey came out of the same world, though for a time lionized, he never surrendered to Vanity Fair.

'In silence and in cunning', Stephen Dedalus would perfect his art. Christy Brown should think upon these things, and turn an angry eye now on the injustices, the poverty and the misery which still exist in the world, from which his own will-power and talent and his gallant family so magnificently rescued him"[7].

* * * *

In 1975 Robert Collis was publishing his autobiography, 'To Be A Pilgrim'. Ironically, he asked the famous author, Christy Brown, to pen the forward. Christy wrote a very short piece, speaking of Collis' many rainbowed life and his friendship with him, "the strange and unique alliance that has deepened over the not unremarkable years of its duration, the impact it has made on his life"[8]. By that stage, Christy had distanced himself from 'the great one' as he had taken to referring to Collis by. He had seen Collis at close quarters for a long period and while admitting that Collis was a great man, he realised that he was not always an admirable person. In "My Left Foot" Christy was careful to document who had done the physical work with him as Collis occasionally overstated his contribution to events. He could be harsh with people, particularly his subordinates. What upset Christy most about Collis, and which was voiced only to a very close friend, was that in his estimation, Collis did not respond in the personal way called upon by a father, in relation to his own handicapped child. Shortly after returning to Ireland, Collis put his son into residential care[9].

As we have seen on his return from Nigeria, Collis resumed his work with the Association for Cerebral Palsy. He was sorely disappointed to find that during his absence, it had not retained its early dynamism. He set about trying to revive it and spent the remaining few years of his life immersed in that task. In the short-term it would appear that he was singularly unsuccessful, but taking a longer view, his efforts paved the way for a major transformation of that organisation.

In 1975 the travail within the Association for Cerebral Palsy became public knowledge when an Annual General Meeting reported on internal dissension. Several newspapers commented on its difficulties. The Irish Times wrote: "The National Association for Cerebral Palsy in Dublin is now operating without a chief executive, a superintendent physiotherapist and a social worker, following a spate of resignations from the professional staff. The Association does work similar to the Central Remedial Clinic... The Cork branch of the Association operates more or less independently. Indeed, the expansion and the success of the Central Remedial Clinic has emphasised the lack of growth in Sandymount. This has been put down to various factors. These include bad communication between the Board and the staff, poor liaison among the staff themselves, lack of publicity about the Association's work, a Board unreceptive to ideas...It has also been said that the Board has insufficient young blood, although the addition of four more Board members has added more life to its activities. The Chairman of the Association, Mr. A.A. Healy, T.D., says that the appointment of a suitable chief executive would solve most of the Association's problems in Sandymount...

The lack of a chief executive is however, the Association's most immediate problem, if the 25 or so children in Bray and 100 or so others in the Sandymount clinic, nursery, school and workshop are to get the deal they deserve. A more vociferous parents association is also vital. Otherwise old rumours about an amalgamation - in effect a take-over - with the Central Remedial Clinic will be revived"[10].

That same year of 1975, saw Collis himself die in a fall from his horse at his farm at Bo Island in county Wicklow. A great life-force disappeared, though it was indeed a fitting way to end a turbulent life. The loss was tragic, especially in the world of rehabilitation, where Collis was introducing a new openness towards creating a national approach, between the Central Remedial Clinic and his own Association of Cerebral Palsy, for services to people with disability. One of his initiatives did bear fruit when the dynamic Lady Valerie Goulding, Co-Founder and Chairman of the Central Remedial Clinic, was invited and accepted an offer to join the Committee of the Eastern Region of Cerebral Palsy Ireland. In the context of the difficulty that voluntary organisations encounter in cooperating with each other, this was a major achievement.

Collis was commemorated in a poem by Christy Brown, which treats of the essence of what Bob Collis was, a great man, giving himself totally to the service of others, with an urgency that did not suffer personages, bureaucrats or mediocrities. The authenticity of the poem, in particular the following four lines, rings true for the author, who had the privilege of knowing and working with Collis for a three year period. These are:

> "You strode rather than stepped through life
> crushing many a demure bloom in your career
> yet with the blunt sensitivity of one
> trading not with images but imperatives".

The complete text of this well-deserved and accurate tribute reads:

> REMEMBERING A FRIEND:
> ROBERT COLLIS
>
> The horse came back alone
> over the morning hills of Wicklow
> no longer bearing its master
> missing the gentle guidance of your hand
> nudging it into homecoming
> mistily wondering perhaps
> why you had stayed behind
> why you had fallen
> so soft and sudden
> to earth
> wordless in the wet grass
> a moment ago you had ridden over like the wind
> surveying your green valley as ever with love.

Down that smoking air a lone calling
hushing your heart in a cloud
bearing you away from the valley and the city
from tenements darkly swarming with stunted life
and sibilant streams and hedges brimming with song
you knew and celebrated with conjoined agony and affection
that sudden swift whisper on the wind
in one swallow rush of zealous possession
stealing your breath past stream and pavement
in that moment out of time
that finds each of us small and alone
though wind and earth and growing things of earth
were brothers to you in that last union
and sang you proud into peace
under a turbulent sky
where your heart's abiding passion lay.

You strode rather than stepped through life
crushing many a demure bloom in your career
yet with the blunt sensitivity of one
trading not with images but imperatives
you were solicitous of mute mayhem
crashing through lives indignant with healing
the arrows of your anger flashing into minds
cramped and closeted in grey contumely of office
physician to the anonymous poor and maimed
loud with tenderness for broken things
making strength and basilicas of belief
out of the deep unsaid sorrows of your life
vain and strong and innocent of malice
and beautiful in the last and only sense.

Friend of all my life
seer of my sapling years
I do not feel your absence as pain
for knowledge of love once gained and given
is never lost or betrayed into unknowing
and there are always rainbows.

* * * *

Christy's next novel was awaited as proof positive as to whether he was again going to contribute to Irish literature, or whether he had succumbed totally to 'Vanity Fair', as Mary Manning had put it. The new novel appeared in 1976, and was called "Wild Grow the Lilies". It carried the dedication "For Mab, Edie, Tulsa and Peach; at the last count, the girls in my life without whom not a single lily would have grown". Christy had said that on occasions he would experience a frenzy of creative activity during which he and his typewriter became one. It was almost like an orgy when inhibition and control did not exist and time meant nothing. He just went on and on writing, writing. He enjoyed these experiences almost as psychedelic happenings.

This might explain the similar verbiage found in the latest work. It too lacked any sign of control with words, which proliferated endlessly. The first page alone contains sentences of eighty one, fifty five and sixty nine words. Later we encounter sentences of over one hundred and even two hundred words. He expects the reader to plod through his meanderings to seek discovery of what could be said in a much more concise form. As Beth Moore said several years earlier, this was bad writing. Understatement was foreign to his style. The story line is that of a bibulous Irish journalist mollocking through a phoney Dublin.

It aims to be bawdy but is merely embarrassing. The hero speaks thus; "Ah yes the Irish Mother is a truly Karmic phenomenon, a continuing emanation and Epiphany of that dark primordial life-force which...". Jeremy Brooks wrote in the Sunday Times of the book; "It's a romp; a long directionless maddening slow romp through bars, beds,'hoors', and phoney aristocrats. The words pour forth endlessly and I'm afraid to no discernible end, unless you're a glutton for Irish garrulity"[11].

Hugh Leonard approached the book with the intention of letting it go to another reviewer, should his opinion prove less than laudatory. But in the end he realised that this would have been cowardly. He found that there was enough sheer joy in the book to compensate for its excesses. He said that "Mr. Brown may lack the snaffle and the reins, but at least he possesses the bloody horse". But before Mr. Leonard penned that finale he found, "The pace is so slow that the reader begins to suspect that the pages are impregnated with marijuana. On page 244 for example, a publican demands an apology from Luke's editor, who has arrived on horseback, and it takes six pages before it is rung out of him...For all heaviness of telling, the book is a slight affair...Too often, one suspects that Mr. Brown is at the mercy of his words, rather than the other way round...It is not the kind of book one gives to a convalescent mammy who is in between Barbara Cartlands. The language is raw; not just near the knuckle but all the way up to the armpit; and the goings-on are such that Mr. Lee Dunne's characters might by comparison be placed alongside Winnie the Pooh...He would achieve twice the effect if he were to half his wordage: but he confuses, I think, volume with content"[12].

Mary Manning wrote of the book: "And wilder and wilder grows Christy Brown's prose style. This intrepid man...has now made the perilous crossing over to Vanity Fair. This is a highly coloured and most deceptive setting, in which the author can only live at second hand. The result is phoney, pretentious and tedious. His latest novel is a pastiche of 'Ulysses in Nightown', Brendan Behan, Sean O'Casey, Lee Dunne and Maria Monk...He should now withdraw from the phoney horny school and be his own man. There is nothing more boring than reading about drunks, sexual frolics in bordellos and literary gents, facetious discourses in bed or out of it...In 'Wild Grow the Lilies' there is no wit, no grace, no beauty...At the end one is tempted to say, "shit up Mr. Brown"[13].

CHAPTER 17

A PERSONAL PORTRAIT : NIALL FALLON ON ' THE CHRISTY BROWNS '.

Though the Browns lived in a remote part of Ireland, they continued to have visitors. Christy still told his very good friends "how dare you be in Kerry and not visit". Dr. Patricia Sheehan visited several times and thoroughly enjoyed herself. She was full of praise for the beautiful home they had created. Ann Jones visited too and was made very welcome. She said that "of course the family felt that they were losing touch with Christy when he went to live in Ballyheigue. But each of the family had to make their own way in life. There were no qualms about that. We all got married and kept in touch with the family. You have to let go sometime".

Another visitor was Fr. Michael Cleary, who was a regular attender at sporting events in Kerry. On one such occasion he was at the nearby Listowel Races when the invitation arrived to visit Mab Cottage. Christy asked him to fulfil a long Irish tradition and celebrate Mass in the house. Christy asked Fr. Cleary to say the Mass for Ma Brown, with just himself and Mary as congregation. Ann Jones had been unaware of this occurrence and was very happy to hear of it, from the author. Fr. Cleary has written of Christy's great faith in God. He also appreciated the sacrifices and effort Mary had made for her husband [1].

The couple themselves travelled widely outside the country, using Cork Airport as their point of exit. They often travelled on the spur of the moment to some event which captured their interest. Christy was so well known everywhere that his presence was an honour for any occasion. The main problem on an on-going basis on these social occasions was Christy's drinking. He had always been fond of drink. But increasingly, as Mary has said, it appeared to be getting out of control[2].

Sean Feehan of Disabled Artists in Cork, proposed compiling a book on the subject of that Association. He wrote to Christy asking for some suitable contribution. At the time the Browns were having some major renovations and an extension done at Ballyheigue.

Christy therefore had great difficulty producing any paintings or suitable photograph. Instead he supplied a written self-portrait of his life, which naturally concentrated mainly on how the Disabled Artists Association, Eric Stegmann and Capt. Feehan had helped him. Painting gave him the opportunity to become self-confident after such an inauspicious start in life. Though more recently he had become better known as a writer, many people still remembered seeing him at work at painting exhibitions in a variety of places round the country. He admits to still having days when it is difficult to motivate himself, but then the beauty of Ballyheigue and his wife Mary inspire him. The document is dated November 1976 and reads;

"I was born in the middle of a large family, 22 in all, in 1932, in the Rotunda Hospital, Dublin. I was, as I later learned, a difficult birth, and almost from the beginning my Mother noticed there was something 'different' about me, though the doctor could detect no abnormality and assured my Mother I was a normal healthy child - an opinion, incidentally, they reversed when I was about nine months old, when they solemnly announced that as far as they could ascertain I was a mental defective and most unlikely to survive into my teens. I am glad to report they were somewhat inaccurate in their prognosis.

I was afflicted with a condition known now universally as Cerebral Palsy, and for which a whole coordinated system of treatment has evolved, but at the time of my birth and for many years afterwards the cause and treatment of this affliction were unknown in medical circles, and because of the outward physical appearance which accompanied the disability many, if not most, sufferers were regarded as being mentally deficient and in danger of being shut away in institutions for the rest of their lives, if the 'authorities' of the day had their way. Lucky for me, my parents were made of sterner stuff and always treated me as just another member of their large unruly brood, subject to the same disciplines and the same penalties if I stepped out of line - speaking very metaphorically, since I could not sit up straight or move or use any of my limbs at all, except one, my left foot, which at the age of nine I suddenly discovered I could use as well as other people use their hands, and with which I later learned to write and paint and so entered a completely new life with almost boundless possibilities for advancement and self-realisation.

Looking back, I find it difficult to remember when I was not painting, and still more difficult to recall when I was not involved with the Disabled Artists' Association, though logic tells me I was about 25 years old when Capt. Sean Feehan of the Mercier Press in Cork first contacted me and asked me if I would like to become a trainee member, with art lessons in my home which the Association would pay for. From then on a whole new world opened up for me and I was soon earning my own living, which of course made all the difference in life to me. Up to then I had been drawing and painting pictures merely as a form of escape from the inner isolation and at times despair which my handicap induced in me; being part of a big family helps, but it is certainly no guarantee that you will be spared the feelings of loneliness and hopelessness which we must confront and endure as we go through life, and as I grew older and more sensitive I subsequently became more aware of the stark unambiguous 'difference' between me and other people. I grew into myself and so used painting, or my own crude attempts at painting, as an escape tunnel which I could use from time to time to break out into a broader, airier world, if only for the time it took me to complete each inexpert picture.

The fact that I was to be actually paid to paint and helped to develop whatever talent I had, produced a startling effect upon my whole personality; my philosophy towards life in general, and my own disability in particular, became brighter, my mind became suffused with hope and rose to all the challenges now suddenly appearing on the horizon. As my self-respect increased so did my confidence, and my pictures became less introverted and cramped and began to express this new buoyancy and delight in being alive in the first place, rather than the mere fact that I was a cripple, which lost most of its old terrible meaning and became almost incidental to the fact that I could now earn my own living.

I began going on painting tours and exhibitions throughout Ireland, organised by the DAA., and though it was somewhat daunting and very much of an ordeal at first, painting before the public did give me added strength and confidence in myself, not just as an artist but as a person, and after the initial shock of "exposure", I soon developed a hardy attitude to my new experience and became so absorbed in my paintings that for the most part I was unaware of all those people crowding the halls and exhibition stands looking on at me as I worked. I was simply earning my bread, doing a job of work, and how I did it was immensely unimportant to me as long as I could personally be satisfied with the result. Not only was it beneficial to my art, but it was an apprenticeship in living and in meeting with people that has stood me in excellent stead ever since.

Meeting Erich Stegmann was one of the truly momentous occasions of my life. It was this unique man's magnanimity of spirit and imagination which first started the original idea of an association to help and promote the work of handicapped artists, and of course it has since spread and grown throughout the world, not only in popular appeal but in artistic stature. Erich Stegmann, being disabled himself, understands the true inner needs and impulses of other handicapped people, but more than this psychological advantage, he is a superb artist whose work, I believe, stands on a par with the great artists of the past as

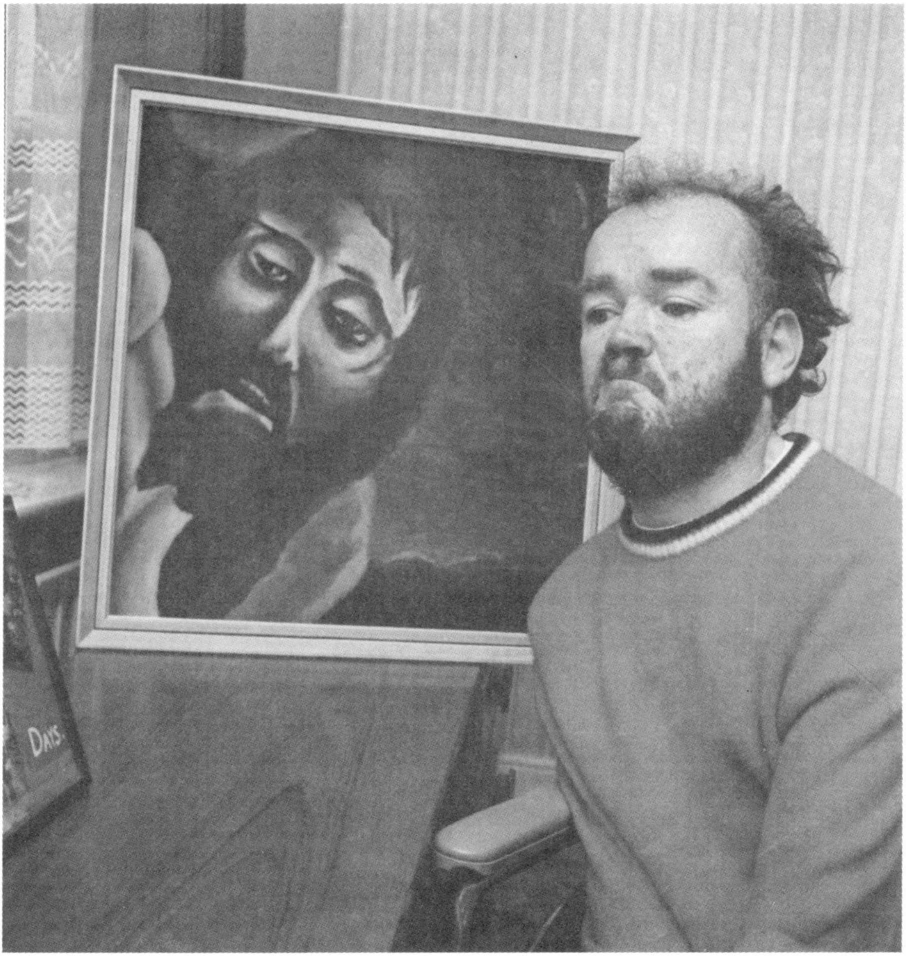

Christy with either a suffering Christ
or a self-portrait
(Courtesy Matthew Walsh)

well as with any artist alive and working today. He speaks no English, but after a few moments in his company this language barrier ceases to matter; his vivid personality and immense zest for living create a kind of aura about him, a sort of magnetic field, so that everyone within range of him is caught up in his charm and propelled along by his own enthusiasm and ebullience. He remains one of the great abiding influences upon my life as man and artist.

It is a great source of comfort and inspiration to me personally to know that the Disabled Artists' Association in Ireland continues to flourish and carry on its splendid work of encouraging other young handicapped people with artistic leanings who, like myself, might otherwise have never found self-independence but for it. It does not deal in idle sympathy nor does it dole out dutiful dollops of charity or compassion; with the DAA one is an artist first and foremost, and a disabled artist secondly, and it is this that distinguishes it and raises it above most other organisations which might have a passing similarity as far as aiding the handicapped is concerned but which fall so far short of the basic philosophy of the DAA. It deals primarily in talent, not loving kindness, and the emphasis is on artists who happen to be handicapped not as artists, but as persons, in a purely physical context. We are after all in the art business, not in the disability stakes, and it is as artists that we want to prove ourselves, not as cripples or wheelchair wizards. The ultimate judgement must be upon what we painted, not how we painted it.

As a writer who has had the incredible and, regrettably, rare good fortune to have gained recognition this side of the grave, my books have travelled the world, and though it might be said to be an increasingly shrinking world, it still gives me great pleasure in knowing that one can still reach out and communicate with people across so many social and ideological continents and divides, through both the printed word and the painted image. In recent times, it is true, my life has become more and more tied to the typewriter rather than the easel as my need for self-expression has shifted more towards the literary form, yet such is the power of the brush, as opposed to the pen, that many people still remember me as a painter rather than a writer and often they ask me whatever happened to that picture they saw me working on a score or more years ago in some parish hall in some unnameable part of the Irish countryside! That kind of thing soon puts my literary pretensions into proper perspective and makes me descend from Parnassus double-quick.

I now live in a most beautiful part of Co. Kerry, with my equally beautiful wife Mary, in a charming country cottage overlooking the Atlantic, a wild, untamed, enchanting corner of the globe where one would have to be a complete and incorrigible dullard not to feel inspired and eager for life at least on most days of the week. Like everyone else this side of paradise, I have my sad, brooding moments when I look out over the splendid panorama of sea and mountain and see only shadows, sorrow, vague portents of doom and melancholy; then I tell myself, what a lovely place to be sad in! It beats the concrete greyness, grime, factory smoke and diesel fumes which formed the backdrop of my growing years, and with lighter heart I turn back to my typewriter or my easel, as might easily be the case. With such living poetry around you wherever your eye turns, it is very hard to translate it all into words or paint, but of course I shall go on trying forever".

The following year Christy was pleased to hear of an Exhibition of paintings and a film which were planned by the Disabled Artists Association involvimg their various Irish members. He wrote to Sean Feehan full of suggestions: "Great news about the proposed exhibition, and of course I'd be delighted to participate and attend. Could you let me know - when you know yourself, of course - exactly what date in March, so that we can make the necessary home arrangements, etc? Also, am I to send the paintings when they are finished on to you in Cork? Please let me know.

I do hope Dr. Hillery can do the opening honours. That would be quite a scoop and quite a boost as well. I also hope the television film turns out well. At least you can't go wrong with the scenery! Talking about filming, if you like we have a rather nice patio here where I paint myself when the weather is kind, commanding a panoramic view over Ballyheigue Bay and the range of mountains beyond, which might come out well on film with Peter Spencer, Pat Casserly and myself working out there. It's just a suggestion that you can ponder in preparing the programme.

I'm hoping that Eric Stegmann can come over. I'm still very disappointed about missing him the last time. It's many years since I last saw Irene Schicker. I look forward to the reunion. As to putting a price tag on the paintings I submitted for the last exhibition, I am really rather hopeless at that kind of thing and prefer to leave it to your own discretion".

The artistic worth of Christy's paintings is, like that of many others, a matter of opinion, taste and possibly fashion. Like most painters only time will tell whether his paintings survive. The publicity engendered by the success of the film, "My Left Foot" in 1988, created a new interest in his paintings. In late 1990, Christies, in association with Hamilton Osborne King of Dublin, put eighteen of them on exhibition at the Royal Hibernian Academy Gallery in Dublin at a major sale of Irish paintings. The Catalogue said, "Stylistically, there is a directness in Brown's work which has nothing to do with naivety. He was a highly sophisticated thinker and his inability to express the complexity of his ideas on canvas must have caused him great frustration. This can be sensed in many of the works which have a vigour and crudity that predates the New Expressionist movement by a decade. It would be difficult to define his influences but he was thoroughly read in art history and there are conscious acknowledgements to masters like Matisse and Cezanne in his work". Niall

Fallon wrote of these paintings: "The Christy Browns, by common consent, were not much more than a fashionable curiosity; lorrying eighteen of them on the market at one time was a decision which backfired, with only eight of the eighteen sold for a total of £15,000"[3].

I think that, even in these days of inflated prices, Christy might have been proud that even one of his paintings fetched £4,200 and another £3,000. He did write at one stage that even if he got master lessons in painting, he realised that he could only ever aspire to be an ordinary painter.

Mab Cottage in Ballyheigue.

CHAPTER 18

' A BLUNT INSTRUMENT ' : A SILVER JUBILEE ; CORK JAZZ FESTIVAL : ' THE SPRING LISTS ' .

Christy settled into country life so completely that he sometimes found it hard to believe how he had lived anywhere else. He had no regrets about leaving "the grey desolate stultifying inertia of Dublin suburban living". As he wrote in September 1977:

"The good news is we're both keeping great and savouring our new rustic existence here with ever increasing delight. While I'm not completely 'rusticated' yet to the extent of chewing hay and counting how many eggs the hens lay each morning, I'm well on the way to becoming thoroughly 'culchified' and very happy about it too. And of course Mary loves it, which makes it all the sweeter.

I came here with all the preoccupations of your average 'townie' and I'm glad to say they've all more or less completely evaporated by now, except the more pleasurable ones.

Workwise I've never been more industrious, though still far from totally chained to the typewriter; indeed, the scenery is so lovely it is often a distraction, so that it often seems almost a shame to waste time on merely literary things. I'm at present embroiled on my fourth novel, which for a change I've set in London of the '60s, the era of Flower Power and Beautiful People and so forth".

He later explained further his reason for such a location when he spoke to the Irish Times, saying that he did not wish to be typecast. He said "I don't want to be another Brendan Behan"[1]. In the same 1977 letter he continued to talk about the novel: "It's taking shape, which is about all I can say about it at the moment. It's a challenge, setting it in London, far from my usual terrain, but I wanted to get right away from the Dublin syndrome for a while and have a go at something entirely different. The other books are all still selling well, so for the moment anyway we're not haunted by the spectre of the workhouse".

His third and last collection of poetry titled, "Of Snails & Skylarks" came out in 1978. It was dedicated to "The inhabitants of Sweetdum". He had always regarded poetry as his best way of communicating. For him poetry was "like a rash": he came out with it almost every day. He thanked God that the rash was incurable. Not surprisingly, his poetry too continued to teem with words, compound adjectival constructions. It was unsophisticated but vigourous and sensual. It was at its best when he wrote of subjects outside himself. But the finesse, the subtlety of that art escaped him. He was incapable of discarding unnecessary words which made his poetry prosaic and full of rhetoric. He was well aware of all this himself. One of these poems is called "A Blunt Instrument" and says:

> "A thing of remorseless gluttony
> of immense invincible vacuity
> is my muse.
>
> Yet it sang once in a rare moment
> a small pure indomitable sound
> escaping from twisted strings
> and somehow after that
> I could almost love the grotesque creature
> as one can sometimes come to love the misbegotten."

Two significant and perhaps inevitable events demonstrated how Christy, so content in his new life, was willing to continue to put space between the present and his past. Dr. Patricia Sheehan decided to celebrate the Silver Jubilee of her involvement with disabled people in October 1977. She intended to gather as many of them as possible together in Dublin to mark the occasion. Her relationship with her patients, as we have continually seen, went far deeper than a mere professional one. She treated all as friends and was a confidant to each as the occasion demanded. They may have been the children she never had. By that stage, Dr. Sheehan had long left the Cerebral Palsy Association, where she felt she and her work were undervalued. She said, sadly, that for some reason, Sandymount was always an unhappy place in her experience. The new building had narrow corridors and low ceilings, which instilled an almost claustrophobic atmosphere. She felt too, that the Board was never in tune with the staff. She believed that because the Board acted purely on an honorary basis, somehow it resented the fact that the staff was paid and consequently never properly valued or respected the people doing the work.

Dr. Sheehan naturally expected that Christy would be the star guest at her Jubilee. She wrote well in advance inviting himself and Mary. To her great disappointment, he declined the invitation, though with his usual gracious style, writing:

“How marvellous to hear from you after so long and more wonderful still to know you’re in such great fettle - more power to you. First the bad news. We almost certainly won’t be able to make it up for your little soiree on October 8th., but we’ll be with you in spirit - whichever way you look at it - and hope the Jubilee festivities go with a bang, as I’m quite sure they will with such a crew in attendance. As you can no doubt imagine, it isn’t easy for us to get up to Dublin very often, what with our two dogs and cat to be tended while we’re gone, as well as numerous other considerations too complicated to go into here - plus the added fact that it’s our 5th wedding anniversary on October 5th. and we might be planning to go abroad somewhere for a couple of days to celebrate that momentous occasion. It might just be Paris - who knows - just to be glaringly and obviously romantic for once in my life. So sadly we must decline your warm invitation and miss the party, but as I say we both wish you all the best and hope your ‘Old Boys’ do you proud and behave like gentlemen.

If you do perchance find yourself in this part of the world don’t dare go back without looking us up - phone number above if you feel like giving us a ring to let us know you’re in the area. It really is incredible to think that so many years have passed since we first met, with so many vast changes, in my case undoubtedly for the better. Mary sends you her warmest regards and best wishes for the success of the get-together on the 8th. Remember me to all my old Bull Alley & Sandymount friends and keep the sacred flag burning.

Good luck in everything you do, Patsy, and love from us both, always”.

Some time later, Katriona Maguire, who had been living for some years with her husband in Brussels, planned to attend the Cork Jazz Festival.(Conor Maguire has presented the very popular jazz programme, ‘In The Mood’ on RTE Radio for several years). She had not seen Christy for a considerable time and felt this might be a suitable opportunity. She knew that he was, like themselves, quite a jazz fan. She wrote and suggested that Mary and Christy might like to come to Cork for the occasion. Failing that, she offered to travel to Kerry to meet them. Much to her disappointment Christy turned down both offers. He said that they were having some work done on the house and they did not want to leave it at that time. This also precluded any visits from friends. This was the only occasion, he ever put Katriona off and she was very saddened by it. She never did visit Ballyheigue.

Both Dr. Sheehan and Katriona Maguire were each in their different ways somewhat surprised and disappointed by Christy’s refusals to meet with them. Both ladies had very long relationships with the Browns. Both had contributed to Christy's development. Katriona had essentially rescued him oblivion and put him in touch with a series of professional people who gave him vital services. Her relationship was entirely altruistic and based on her deep Christianity and humanity. Dr. Sheehan's introduction to Christy was that of a professional who later became a personal friend. Her relationship always retained part of the professional aura, which afforded her some distance as between doctor and patient. For both women, Christy's success was wonderful. But it would have been more difficult for them to realise that they too were part of a past, he was anxious to put behind him. Once he left Sandymount he never revisited the place. He was a bird in flight who was interested in new horizons. He was a man who had the facility for making the hard decision. Both ladies had witnessed earlier examples of this and they did not begrudge him his freedom; rather they gloried in it.

The novel-in-progress continued to be the most difficult Christy had ever written. He became depressed by the whole exercise. Eventually he found himself having to go to a third draft. He began to regret ever having started it, realising that he did not have the required background, for it to be credible. His main consolation was a new typewriter which could erase at the touch of a key. His schedule of work was to try to complete about two thousand words daily.

Eventually in November 1979 he reported getting the book finished.

He wrote to Peter Sheridan:

"Things have been piling up on top of me and what with getting the book finished at last and putting off the awful job of editing the script for as long as possible - never mind re-reading the bloody thing. I just haven't been in the right frame of mind for letter writing or much else for that matter. In fact what editing has been done is harmless and hence the publication date is something that at the moment seems like millions of light - or heavy - years away, though I like to be optimistic and think that it will be sometime in early 1980, perhaps for the spring lists.

I'm not really worried by the time factor now that I've got the thing finished - the important thing now is the rewriting and belting it into final shape before it leaves my sight. After almost four years of writing it, the thought of another couple of months trimming and pruning the brute isn't all that daunting after all".

There had long been talk of adapting 'Down All the Days' as a play or a film script. The Abbey Theatre was interested in the project and Peter Sheridan had

OSCAR THEATRE

Presents
THE WORLD PREMIERE OF

DOWN ALL THE DAYS

By
CHRISTY BROWN
Adapted by
PETER SHERIDAN

"Cry then, with the weeping stars from the debris of your life. Cry then, for the unnamable things, unnamably lost down all the speechless years."

worked on an adaptation for the stage. The Abbey was to produce the play but then Joe Dowling, Artistic Director of the Abbey, decided to defer it. Christy wrote to Peter Sheridan:

"I did get a very nice friendly letter from Joe Dowling explaining the reasons for deferring the play, and I fully agree. No point in going ahead until we get the best possible cast for the job. Snag is - we probably won't be here when it comes on! No alarm bells, however...".

CHAPTER 19

A STRANGE TRANSFER : ALCOHOLISM : ' A PROMISING CAREER ' : COLLABORATING WITH THE SHERIDANS : A LAST MEETING .

Fate and circumstances led to Christy and Mary deciding to leave Kerry. They had been very happy there, in a location of startling natural beauty overlooking Ballyheigue Bay and the Dingle Peninsula. But local difficulties led them to decide to move, not just out of Kerry, but out of Ireland, on a temporary basis.

As Christy wrote to Peter Sheridan: "We're leasing a cottage in Somerset in fact, only across the duckpond, for a few months while trying to find some place here on the east coast to live, having made up our minds to move from Kerry for a number of reasons with which I won't bore you right now".

They had been on a motoring holiday in the West country earlier and thought it beautiful. Christy hoped it would prove stimulating and believed that, "a change was as good as a rest and nothing ever remained static. The West country is a beautiful part of England and the change in scenery and environment etc. should be interesting and in its own way stimulating. Bristol is not that far from where we'll be staying so we can easily get a plane back whenever the play comes on". He hoped to move early in the new year.

Luckily Christy was well off, having taken good advice on investments. As he said himself, he no longer had to worry about the annual increase in the price of Guinness. He was very aware as a disabled man that money could starkly spell out the difference between acceptable living or hell on earth, between the need and desire to live or the bitter craving after death, the almost sensuous temptation of suicide. Then, most of all, he was glad they could afford to move as the spirit took them.

It was a major wrench for Christy to leave Ireland. Many of his friends and admirers thought it a mistake. They saw it as another move away from his roots. Dr. Sheehan believed that Christy needed the stimulation of being continually able to observe people. To expect him to be able to write without that observation, she felt was unrealistic. The move to Glastonbury, she deemed an awful cross. Their new home, a cottage, stood in its own very spacious grounds in the village of Parbrook, North Glastonbury in Somerset. Mary had an aunt living in the area which, was a positive thing. Mary believed that there was less prejudice against disabled people in England. Christy continued work on editing his novel. But his heart was not in it. He was not proud of it[1]. Parbrook was a beautiful spot but it soon became apparent that it was not right for Christy. There were no working-class people there. It was very to-the-manor-born type of country. They found the people very dour. The English public house hours confused him. Being a total stranger in the area and deprived of any regular visitors, he began to drink heavily at home. All the fun seemed to be going out of his life.

Gradually Christy's drinking became more uncontrollable. Mary has said, "He was an alcoholic. He needed to drink, no two ways about it. He was alright when he was working, but when we moved to Somerset, it got worse because he was so lonely and couldn't stand the weird pub hours. He was really in a very bad way. The brain, everything was going - he was drinking brandy at breakfast time, not eating. He had become a danger to himself, so that it was a relief when the doctor took him into hospital to dry out. I wondered why I was not strong enough to keep him off it"[2]. Christy finally finished the novel to his satisfaction and sent it off to his publishers. The book was dedicated "To my Friend and Editor David Farrer, I hope his patience will be rewarded".

This clearly signalled Christy's own doubts about the latest enterprise[3]. This novel was published posthumously in August 1982 with a companion volume of Collected Poetry. Once again the critics were placed in a dilemma, though this time they had the added burden of passing judgement on the work of a deceased Christy Brown. But they rose to the occasion with sentiments such as ," but it would be far shabbier to pretend that this book constitutes a fitting conclusion to his extraordinary literary career. Misconceived, overwritten and (eventually) carelessly edited, it might more kindly have been allowed to perish with him", wrote Nicholas Shrimpton in the Sunday Times[4]. Christy himself would not have been surprised by the critical reaction to the 'brute' he had found so difficult to write.

It was quite apparent that the author did not have the background to adequately portray the milieu of a bourgeois childhood in South London and a subsequent contemporary pop music scene. The same overlong descriptive passages recur. It was no surprise that one reviewer wrote, "Had this been a first novel, the verdict would probably have been 'promising' and extended itself to a recognition of the unusual potential inherent in that promise"[5].

In Dublin agreement had finally been reached to produce Peter Sheridan's stage adaptation of 'Down All the Days', under a new production team. Christy had been very particular about the project. He had sent back Sheridan's first script, asking for a reworking of same. He was very pleased with the result. This used a narrator to verbalise the imaginings and thoughts of the young Christy. He found the second script very theatrical and a good job, realising that the task could not have been easy. Early in 1981 Christy wrote to Peter Sheridan apologising that it took him so long to write saying:

"Sorry it's taken me so long to write in answer to all the glad tidings that have been emanating from Ballybough recently, but it's a long and by no means edifying story so let's skip it and just concentrate on the good news for once - a welcome change. Matter of fact Chris O'Neill just phoned - a few minutes ago - to say they plan on putting on the play on either the 29th or 30th of April at the Oscar and hoping that we'll be able to make it over either for rehearsals or opening night. We'll do our level best to be there, of course, but I've quite a bit on my plate at present, as Mary may have told you on the phone. However all depends on my work-rate and since I've gone easy on the booze, I should be able to meet commitments here on time and make it over. Needless to say we'd both love to be there on the night - nothing like it in the world, or so I believe. Chris O'Neill said he'll be sending me on the contract tomorrow or the next day, plus 'the readies', so all seems set fair. He sounds a nice enough bloke and seems very keen on the production. I'm glad we're sticking to the original Abbey script; I honestly don't think we could improve on it. As soon as you can, will you give me some idea of the cast, especially who is playing the Father.

When I write again or better still if we see you in Dublin I'll unreel you a little more footage-! - of how things have been with me since we last met. Meanwhile it's back to the grindstone after too long an absence and fervently hoping we'll make it over for the storming of the citadel. My regards to the brother and wife and Mary sends her love".

The play opened at the Oscar in Ballsbridge at the end of April. It was directed by Jim Sheridan, Peter's brother. Christy contributed a programme note saying: "I am delighted at the prospect of breaking into drama. I am very pleased at the adaptation by Peter Sheridan. We both collaborated on the script and I am very happy with the result that Peter has come up with. He has captured the spirit of my novel 'Down all the Days' succinctly. My career has taken a new dimension in theatre and I hope to continue in that medium. Whilst my novels and poetry take much of my time the prospect of theatre excited and enthrals me". Among the cast were, Tom Murphy, Garrett Keogh, Geraldine Plunkett, Marie Conmee, Vincent Smith, Laurie Morton and Shane Connaughton.

Old Oscar Theatre; is now a religious centre.

Though the Oscar theatre was only a few hundred yards away from Christy's old Alma Mater, Cerebral Palsy's Sandymount School & Clinic, it was the Irish Wheelchair Association on the north side of the city which benefited from the Premiere. Katriona Maguire happened to be at home in Wicklow on a weeks holiday from Brussels, when she noticed on the Evening Herald that the play was opening that very night. She came to the Oscar in the hope of meeting members of the Brown family, including Christy and Mary. As the curtain went up, she was disappointed that there was no sign of either of the latter pair. But at the interval they both arrived, having just flown in from London. Katriona was told that Christy had been in hospital.

After the show they all adjourned to Ryans public house on Sandymount Green, where they spent an enjoyable few hours. Later that night Katriona drove Christy and Mary into town where they were staying at the Gresham Hotel. It had been a bitter-sweet meeting for Katriona. She never saw him again. The play received pretty favourable reviews. Deaglan De Bhreadun wrote, "It is not an easy book to adapt for the stage. Peter Sheridan employs a narrator, whom among other things informs us of the innermost thoughts of the crippled boy, who is the central character. The device is not entirely successful...The Father is a fascinating character in his own right - An uneven production then, but one which should be seen"[6]. Ann Jones says that as far as she could gather, Christy did not like the play. She herself found it an emotional experience.

That same days Irish Times carried a long interview with Christy, conducted in the Sandymount public house, as he sipped Jameson through a plastic straw. In it he plays the 'broth of a boy' character, hard drinking, boastful, arrogant, who alternates between his homes in Glastonbury and Ballyheigue. He did not miss Dublin, saying it wasn't the same now. The 'crack' was only a distraction from writing. He regarded his first book as 'trite'. His first play, which he disowned, had been produced by Mme. Bannard in a Mount Street basement. "Thank God its not around anymore" he said, adding that he had plenty more plays under the bed, which was what he hoped to be doing for the future[7].

CHAPTER 20.

SUDDEN DEATH : INQUEST ' WELCOME HOME CHRISTY ': THE FOUR BLESSINGS OF CHRISTY BROWN .

The Browns intended to return to Ireland and had made tentative plans to do so for the Spring of 1982. Though he had earlier written a poem titled, "A Better Than Death Wish", in which he said:

> "O God...
> Grant me this ;
> That when I die
> it will be under an Irish sky",

This wish was not to be fulfilled. On Sunday evening of 6 September 1981 Mary and Christy had been watching a video of that years Wimbledon tennis finals. Mary had prepared a meal of roast lamb for their dinner. She began to feed her husband as usual. At one stage she left him alone for a few moments. When she returned she found him in distress[1]. He looked pale and there was a rattle in his throat. Then he went purple and she telephoned for an ambulance[2]. Mary did what she could then, but had to wait until a doctor arrived from ten miles away. She believed that he was alive when the ambulance man arrived and tried to dislodge something from his throat. "To see someone die in front of you...it's terrible", Mary said[3].

Christy's sudden death was headlined in newspapers in Ireland and reported widely around the world. His brother, Sean, travelled from London to Somerset, as soon as he heard the news. He made a statement, saying about the death, "his wife was feeding him his meal and he had some difficulty swallowing. Medical help arrived but he was dead leaving the house"[4]. Mr. Brown also said that there was no question of his brother having choked on a bone, but the actual cause of death would have to wait the result of the medical examination. Because of the suddenness of death, an inquest had to be held to determine the cause of death. Mona Byrne was devastated to hear of her brother's death. Her understanding of what happened was, "He choked to death. Christy was a person who had a very small swallow, and you know the head would jerk back with the cerebral palsy. If he was swallowing something, if it stuck there and the head went back, naturally it would be all over in a second. I presume that's what happened".

In Ballyheigue, where the local Pattern was taking place, an old friend of Christy's, Donal Leane, said, "Flags will be flying at half mast in respect for Christy, who in the five years they lived here, became one of the village's deepest and loyal friends and for whom all the local people had an almighty regard and trust". At the inquest, Mary said that Christy had drunk " quite a bit of vodka" and on the Sunday he had a bottle of red wine and some brandy. She gave him two sleeping pills that evening. The Mendip coroner, Mr. J. Fenton-Rutter, asked if she knew that sometimes drink and pills could be a dangerous combination, resulting in vomiting and asphyxiation. Mary said that she was so aware, but that her husband had been "very strong before", adding, "I thought by giving him sleeping pills it would let him sleep for a few hours and not have anymore alcohol, which was the demon of the case, if you like"[5].

The pathology report attributed death to "shock and asphyxiation due to the impaction of food in the larynx"[6]. The coroner ruled that Mr. Brown died from shock and asphyxiation, as a result of choking on food. He recorded a verdict of death by misadventure[7].

Mr. Fenton-Rutter offered his sympathy to Mrs Brown. She obviously looked after the author very well, he said. Mrs Brown sat, near to tears, in the public benches with other relatives to hear the coroner record his verdict[8]. The delay caused by the need for the inquest, added to the trauma for the entire family, especially for those living in Dublin.

Christy's body arrived back to Dublin Airport on a Friday afternoon. Mary had flown directly into Cork Airport and gone to Ballyheigue for the weekend. Dr. Sheehan, who heard of the death while in Lourdes, was back in Dublin for the funeral. She went to Dublin airport and was on hand at the terminal building, as Christy's body was wheeled out to be handed over to the waiting undertakers. She put a hand on the coffin and said, "welcome home Christy". The coffin was then removed to Massey's funeral parlour in Thomas Street, where the family and friends were waiting. Everyone paid their respects as prayers were said.

That same evening, after her medical duties, Dr. Sheehan managed to get to Masseys a few minutes before closing time. All the mourners had gone. The attendant told her she could go upstairs for a moment before he locked up. The first thing she noticed about Christy was his straight jaw. It had always been slightly crooked in life. He was dressed in a brocaded shroud with no religious emblems. She them remembered that she had two Rosary Beads with her. One had come from Lourdes and had a drop of Lourdes holy water incased behind the cross. This Rosary Beads she placed in the coffin beside his left foot, said a prayer and left.

The next day, Saturday, many thousands of people, the author included, went to pay their last respects to Christy Brown as he lay in his open coffin. There were no burials on a Saturday or Sunday, so the funeral had to wait until Monday. Katriona Maguire was in Lourdes at this time and sent her daughter to the funeral obsequies.

Ann Jones organised the religious part of the proceedings. She contacted Fr. Michael Cleary and asked him to officiate at the funeral Mass. St. Bernadette's Church, Clogher Road, Crumlin had been Christy's parish church. It was there a solemn sung Mass was celebrated on the Monday morning. The church was packed with family friends and admirers. The President of Ireland was represented by his ADC, Colonel Stephen Timmons. The Lord Mayor of Dublin, Alexis Fitzgerald, attended. An Taoiseach was also represented. Local members of Dail Eireann and other dignitaries were also present. Much to many peoples' surprise, and to the regret of the Brown family, Christy's body remained in the funeral parlour and was not brought to church[9].

Dr. Sheehan read the Lesson and chose chapter twenty one, verses one to six from the Apocalypse of St. John. It began, "then I saw a new heaven and a new earth...I am the Alpha and the Omega, the Beginning and the End. I will give water from the well of life free to anybody who is thirsty". Local schoolchildren sung at the Mass, miming the Our Father. One girl sang 'Nearer My God to Thee'; another sang 'Going Home'. Fr. Cleary spoke about Christy and the people who had assisted him on his journey through life.

He noted that 1981 was The Year of the Disabled, saying how Christy had given so much hope to disabled people throughout the world. He said that Christy had four great blessings. The first was his sense of humour, which could make a laugh out of many of his great frustrations. Another was his mother, a great hardy little woman, whose stubbornness and patience and faith, discovered and released her son's spirit. His third blessing was Dr. Bob Collis who looked after him medically and directed his reading and writing. His fourth blessing, Fr. Cleary said, was almost a miracle. He met a lovely girl, Mary, who saw through the distorted body someone she loved, and they got married.

Mary had been on her way to Dublin that morning by train. The train had broken down at Portlaoise about sixty miles from Dublin. She was continuing her journey by taxi and had sent a message to the undertakers to delay the funeral until she arrived. After the Mass, the mourners made their way from the church in Crumlin into Thomas Street to Massey's, to discover that there was going to be a delay. This lasted for about ninety minutes.

Dr. Sheehan had driven directly from Crumlin to Glasnevin and couldn't understand what was causing the delay. Eventually she had to leave to attend an afternoon clinic and missed the burial. When Mary did arrive the cortege was given a police escort, to get it to Glasnevin as quickly as possible. On arrival there, it was discovered that the gravediggers were on their lunch break.

St. Paul's, Glasnevin Cemetery.

Frantic efforts were made to locate them. Eventually they emerged into the heavy drizzling rain to assist with the burial. By that time the gathering around the coffin was quite small, composed of the family and a few ardent admirers, including Fr. Cleary, Ulick O'Connor, Eamon MacThomais, Anna Manahan, Pat Casserly, Noel Pearson, Chris O'Neill, all determined to see Christy buried in the earth. At the graveside, Mary sobbed quietly, unable to speak.

Ulick O'Connor wrote that, "none of his English acquaintances were at the grave; his publishers had done well out of him. One wonders what was he doing in Somerset anyway? He had torn himself from the tribe - But you had to come back in the end"[10].

Brendan Kennelly thought that Christy's emergence as a writer was "miraculous". He saw him as a poet who wrote novels and that it was his poetic gift of insight and language that made his novels special. Others would claim that from a literary point of view, only 'Down All the Days' has any real merit, arguing that the absence of Beth Moore or some other such strong person with a critical literary facility, was never compensated for. It must also be recognised that the probability is, that once Christy tasted the fruits of 'Vanity Fair', nobody could deflect him from travelling down that road. However Kennelly, a distinguished poet himself and Professor of English at Trinity College, Dublin, thought Brown had a "true lyrical appreciative nature" and even when his poems were technically deficient, they still managed to be attractive. He thought Christy's love poetry especially good, because he recognised and analysed the shadows that sometimes obscure the sun of love. Kennelly wrote, "To put it bluntly, Christy Brown was, above all, an honest writer - an honest writer with a deep-seated lyrical gift, but he also had a great ear for Dublin dialogue and it is this combination of lyricism, realistic dialogue, psychological insight and unfailing humour that placed him in the line of Beckett, O'Casey, Joyce and Behan"[11].

Writing to the author in October 1988, Hugh Leonard was of the opinion that, "Christy Brown was not nearly so good a writer as Christopher Nolan and that his handicap was probably taken into account by critics. Probably Christy resented this, but it was unavoidable".

Christy Brown certainly had literary talent. He proved that with his masterpiece, 'Down All the Days'. But unfortunately it became a talent dissipated in a not dissimilar fashion, to that of another Crumlin man, Brendan Behan. Christy was catapulted into fame much too soon, before he was sophisticated enough to deal with the exploiters of innocence. Notoriety claims a price, often an inordinant one, and it is difficult to ward it off and to work at one's craft "in silence and cunning". His wife, Mary, certainly tried her best to protect him and provide a good writing environment. But despite what his artistic legacy may be, one still has to remember above all, that the odyssey of his short forty nine year life, was and will remain one of the most inspiring and heart-warming stories of twentieth century Ireland. As he interrupted Ulick O'Connor in 1972 to tell a gathering that his mother was not dead, that she was there among them, so too, may we say that Christy Brown is not dead. He remains with us, a continuing source of inspiration.

Nebulae Numbed Birth

Firstly may I say, Christy Brown
I loudly laud you for pioneering
Nasty niches of poisonous terrain
In your search for an escape route
For brain damaged man.

I nobly salute
Natures noblesse of creativity
As expressed in your lyrical musings.
Regretfully we never met
But memory of nodding acquaintance
With savage, pathetic man's
Indifference to our common plight
Coupled with dank death's call
To you on my birthday
Makes brothers of two anointed ones.

Christopher Nolan.

AUTHOR'S NOTE

When Christy Brown died in 1981, I was Principal Teacher at Cerebral Palsy Ireland's Sandymount School-Clinic for some years. I felt that we should remember him and organised a traditional Month's Mind Mass at the School. Many of his family and friends joined pupils and staff for the Service. I undertook to further commemorate Christy at a later stage.

In 1988 I organised a 'Christy Brown Commemorative Day' at Sandymount. This consisted of a Mass, a series of readings from his work by pupils and staff, including Dr. Mary O'Donnell, and a Memorial Lecture, by Dr. Patricia Sheehan. Again this was attended by a large gathering of his family and friends. It was as a result of this function that I acquired a large collection of Christy Brown's letters.

A pictorial portrait of Christy Brown hangs in Sandymount and our School library is named after him. Robert Collis, the founder of Cerebral Palsy Ireland, is also remembered by a pictorial portrait. In latter years, the Association he founded, has developed into a vibrant national voluntary organisation, of which he would be most proud. Its centre in Tralee is called, 'The Christy Brown Centre'

Notes and References

CHAPTER NOTES

CHAPTER ONE

1. Dillon TWT. Studies, Vol. 24, no. 133, March 1945. p.19. Slum Clearance Past and Present.
2. Collis WRF. The State of Medicine in Ireland Carmichael Prize Essay.

CHAPTER TWO

1. A Wonderful Woman Reality 1990 Moira Lysaght.

CHAPTER THREE

1. Interview with Katriona Maguire 1989.

CHAPTER FOUR

1. Collis WRF Carmichael Prize Essay
2. Letter from James Staunton, Bishop of Ferns and Secretary to the Irish Catholic Hierarchy, to John A Costello, Taoiseach, 11 October 1955.
3. To Be A Pilgrim Autobiography of Robert Collis Secker & Warburg 1975 pp.91-95.
4. ibid
5. To Be A Pilgrim op. cit. pp.91-95.

CHAPTER FIVE

1. To Be A Pilgrim op. cit. p.19.
2. One Hundred Years of Irish Rugby Edmund Van Esbeck Gill & MacMillan 1974 p.187.
3. Interview with Alex Comfort by Des Nix Sunday Press 1988.
4. To Be A Pilgrim op. cit. p.77.
5. Masters, Midwives And Ladies-In-Waiting The Rotunda Hospital 1745-1995 A & A Farmer 1995 p.136.
6. Irish Journal of Medical Science 1944 pp.355.365 Paediatric Department.
7. Collis WRF aand Mary O'Donnell Cerebral Palsy Archives of Diseases in Childhood Vol. 26, No. 129, Oct. 1951. British Medical Association London p. 395.
8. ibid p. 387.

CHAPTER SIX

1. Interview by Author 1989,
2. Collis & O'Donnell op. cit. pp. 396-7.

CHAPTER SEVEN

1. To Be A Pilgrim op, cit. p135.
2. My Left Foot Christy Brown p. 165.
3. To Be A Pilgrim op. cit. p.135.
4. In Interview with Author
5. Ibid.
6. Original with Author.
7. To Be A Pilgrim op. cit. p.136.
8. The Word May 1972. Des Rushe interviews Christy Brown
9. To Be A Pilgrim op. cit. p. 134.

CHAPTER EIGHT

1. To Be A Pilgrim op. cit. p. 97.
2. Masters, Midwives.. op. cit. p.122.
3. ibid. p.136.
4. To Be A Pilgrim op. cit. p.143.
5. ibid. p. 152.
6. ibid. p. 154.

CHAPTER NINE

1. Four Blessings of Christy Brown Fr. Michael Cleary Sunday Independent 13 September 1981.

CHAPTER ELEVEN

1. Sunday Times Anne Spackman 23 December 1984.

CHAPTER TWELVE

1. Ireland A Social and Cultural History Terence Brown Fontana 1985 p. 160.
2. Word Interview op. cit.
3. Interview with author.

CHAPTER THIRTEEN

1. It Started on the Late Late Show Pam Collins Ward River Press 1981. pp.46-47.
2. The Guiding Light op. cit.
3. The Times London 1970.
4. To Be A Pilgrim op. cit. 234.
5. Irish Independent 16 May 1970.
6. Irish Times Niall Fallon 25 May 1970.

CHAPTER FOURTEEN

[1]. Sunday Times 25 January 1970.
[2]. 23/01/1970 & 01/04/1990.
[3]. Sunday Times 1 April 1990.
[4]. Irish Times 25 September 1971.
[5]. Word Interview op. cit.
[6]. In interview with author.

CHAPTER FIFTEEN

[1]. Readers Digest 'Unforgettable Christy Brown' July 1982. p. 116.
[2]. Word Interview op. cit.

3. Sunday Independent Interview with Mary Brown by Mary McAnally-Burke
3 September 1989.

[4]. Irish Times Interview with Mary Brown by Michael Dwyer 26 March 1990.
[5]. Word Interview op. cit.
[6]. To Be A Pilgrim op. cit. p 235.

CHAPTER SIXTEEN

[1]. Irish Times Interview 26 March 1990.
[2]. Irish Times Interview 16 January 1990.
[3]. Sunday Independent 3 September 1989.
[4]. ibid
[5]. Irish Times interview 26 March 1990.
[6]. A Shadow on Summer Christy Brown Secker 1974.
[7]. Irish Times 3 August 1974.
[8]. To Be A Pilgrim op. cit. p. 1X.
[9]. ibid. p. 230
[10]. Irish Times 1 October 1975.
[11]. Sunday Times 11 April 1976.
[12]. Sunday Independent 10 April 1976.
[13]. Irish Times 16 April 1976.

CHAPTER SEVENTEEN

[1]. Sunday Independent 10 September 1981.
[2]. Irish Times 26 March 1990.
[3]. Irish Times 15 December 1990.

CHAPTER EIGHTEEN

[1]. Irish Times 1 May 1981.

CHAPTER NINETEEN

[1]. Irish Times interview 26 March 1990.
[2]. Sunday Independent interview 3 September 1989.
[3]. Irish Times 26 March 1990.
[4]. Sunday Times 8 August 1982.
[5]. Irish Independent Gerry Colgan 21 August 1982.
[6]. Irish Times 1 May 1981.
[7]. ibid.

CHAPTER TWENTY

[1]. Irish Independent 10 September 1981.
[2]. ibid.
[3]. Irish Times Interview 26 March 1990.
[4]. Irish Times 8 September 1981.
[5]. Evening Press 9 September 1981.
[6]. ibid
[7]. Irish Independent 10 September 1981.
[8]. Irish Times 10 September 1981.
[9]. Irish Times 15 September 1981.
[10]. Irish Times 15 September 1981.
[11]. Irish Independent 8 September 1981.

INDEX